BUSINESS ENGLISH SHORT STORIES FOR B1 ENGLISH LEARNERS

50 Engaging Workplace Tales to Enhance Your Communication Skills

Elizabeth Snow

CONTENTS

Title Page
1.	1
The Email Dilemma	2
2.	6
The Big Presentation	7
3.	11
Meeting Madness	12
4.	16
The Office Gossip	17
5.	21
Customer Complaints	22
6.	26
The Job Interview	27
7.	31
The Miscommunication	32
8.	36
The Product Launch	37
9.	41
The Difficult Client	42
10.	46

The First Day	47
11.	51
The Office Party	52
12.	56
The Elevator Pitch	57
13.	61
The Team Leader	62
14.	67
The Conference Call	68
15.	72
The Contract Negotiation	73
16.	78
The Office Politics	79
17.	83
The Dress Code	84
18.	88
The Promotion	89
19.	93
The Networking Event	94
20.	98
The Tight Deadline	99
21.	103
The Client Presentation	104
22.	108
The Proposal	109
23.	113
The International Meeting	114
24.	118

The Office Move	119
25.	124
The Conflict Resolution	125
26.	129
The Budget Meeting	130
27.	135
The Brainstorming Session	136
28.	141
The Sales Pitch	142
29.	147
The Annual Review	148
30.	152
The Business Trip	153
31.	157
The New Policy	158
32.	162
The Product Feedback	163
33.	167
The Sustainability Initiative	168
34.	173
The Training Session	174
35.	178
The Office Redesign	179
36.	183
The Diversity Workshop	184
37.	189
The Time Management Challenge	190
38.	194

The Customer Survey	195
39.	199
The Corporate Social Responsibility Project	200
40.	204
The Public Relations Crisis	205
41.	209
The Market Research	210
42.	214
The Office Ergonomics	215
43.	219
The Mentorship Program	220
44.	224
The Innovation Challenge	225
45.	229
The Office Charity Drive	230
46.	234
The Health and Safety Training	235
47.	239
The Performance Metrics	240
48.	244
The Company Merger	245
49.	249
The Product Launch Event	250
50.	254
The Annual Report	255

1.

THE EMAIL DILEMMA

Sarah sat at her desk, tapping her fingers on the keyboard, staring at the blank email draft on her computer screen. She had to send an important message to her boss, Mr. Thompson, but no matter how hard she tried, she couldn't find the right words. The project she was managing had hit a snag, and now there was a delay that she needed to explain.

She typed, "Dear Mr. Thompson," and then deleted it immediately. "No, that sounds too formal," she thought. She tried again: "Hi Mr. Thompson," but that felt too casual. She sighed, feeling the pressure of the ticking clock.

Sarah knew she needed to strike the right balance in her tone—professional yet approachable, honest but not overly negative. The last thing she wanted was to sound incompetent or unprepared. She had already spent the past thirty minutes writing and erasing, and the anxiety was building.

Just then, her colleague Jason walked by and noticed her frustration. "Hey Sarah, everything okay?" he asked.

Sarah looked up and groaned, "I'm trying to write this email to Mr. Thompson about the delay, but I just can't get it right. I don't want to sound like I'm making excuses, but I also don't want to be too harsh on myself."

Jason nodded sympathetically. "I get it. Writing these kinds of emails can be tricky. Why don't you start by explaining the situation clearly, then suggest a solution? That way, you're being transparent but also showing that you're on top of things."

Sarah considered Jason's advice. She realized that her approach had been too focused on trying to sound perfect, rather than simply communicating the facts. Taking a deep breath, she started typing:

"Dear Mr. Thompson,

I hope this message finds you well. I wanted to inform you about a recent development in our project. We encountered an unexpected issue with one of our key suppliers, which has unfortunately caused a delay in our timeline. However, I have already reached out to a backup supplier, and we should be able to get back on track within the next two days.

Please let me know if you have any questions or would like to discuss this further.

Best regards, Sarah"

Sarah read through the email and felt a wave of relief. It was clear, polite, and professional. She wasn't hiding the problem, but she was also taking responsibility and offering a solution.

Jason glanced over her shoulder and smiled. "Looks good, Sarah. You nailed it."

Feeling much better, Sarah hit "Send" and leaned back in her chair. She realized that the key to writing effective emails wasn't just about choosing the right words, but also about being clear and straightforward. In the end, it was more about communication than perfection.

Later that afternoon, she received a reply from Mr. Thompson:

"Thank you for the update, Sarah. I appreciate your quick action to resolve the issue. Keep me posted on any further developments."

Sarah smiled. The email had gone better than she expected. From then on, she approached her emails with more confidence, knowing that clear communication was always the best strategy.

Approachable - Friendly and easy to talk to.
- Mr. Thompson is very approachable, so Sarah felt comfortable discussing the issue with him.

Balance - A situation in which different elements are equal or in the correct proportions.
- Sarah needed to find the right balance between being professional and approachable.

Competent - Having the necessary skills and knowledge to do something successfully.
- Sarah didn't want to appear incompetent when explaining the project delay.

Consider - To think about something carefully before making a decision.
- Sarah considered Jason's advice before rewriting her email.

Development - A new event or change that is likely to affect a situation.
- Sarah informed her boss about the recent development in the project.

Expect - To believe that something will happen or is likely to happen.
- Sarah expected a response from Mr. Thompson by the end of the day.

Issue - An important topic or problem that people are discussing or debating.

- The team encountered an issue with their key supplier, causing a delay.

Polite - Having or showing good manners and respect for other people.

- Sarah made sure her email was polite and respectful.

Professional - Relating to or connected with a profession.

- Sarah needed to maintain a professional tone in her email.

Relief - A feeling of reassurance and relaxation following release from anxiety or distress.

- Sarah felt a huge relief after sending the email.

2.

THE BIG PRESENTATION

Tom sat at his desk, staring at the stack of papers in front of him. His hands were slightly trembling as he reviewed the notes for his upcoming presentation. Tomorrow, he would have to stand in front of the entire office and present their new marketing strategy to a potential client. The thought made his heart race.

Tom had never been fond of public speaking. In fact, he usually avoided it whenever possible. But this time, he couldn't say no. His boss, Ms. Parker, had specifically chosen him for the task, saying that his knowledge of the project made him the best person to present it. Despite her confidence in him, Tom couldn't shake off the nervousness.

As he practiced his speech, Tom's mind kept drifting to all the things that could go wrong. What if he forgot his lines? What if the client didn't like the proposal? What if he completely embarrassed himself?

The next day arrived faster than Tom had hoped. Dressed in his best suit, he entered the conference room, where the client and several of his colleagues were already seated. The room felt cold and intimidating. Tom took a deep breath, trying to calm his nerves.

Ms. Parker gave him an encouraging smile as she introduced him to the client. "Tom here has been working closely on this project and has some great insights to share," she said.

Tom nodded and approached the front of the room. His hands were still shaking, but he managed to keep a firm grip on his notes. He began his presentation, speaking slowly at first, careful to articulate each word.

As he continued, Tom noticed something surprising—people were paying attention. The client was nodding along, and his colleagues were taking notes. Encouraged by this, Tom found his voice becoming stronger and more confident. He started to move away from his notes and speak more naturally, explaining the strategy with enthusiasm.

By the time he finished, the nervousness that had plagued him was gone. The client smiled and asked a few questions, which Tom answered with ease. Ms. Parker even gave him a thumbs-up from the back of the room.

After the meeting, the client expressed how impressed he was with the presentation. "You've made a strong case for your strategy, Tom. I look forward to working with you," he said.

Tom couldn't believe it. Not only had he managed to get through the presentation without any major mistakes, but he had also won over the client. It was a moment of triumph that he hadn't expected.

Later that day, Ms. Parker approached him with a big smile. "I knew you could do it, Tom. You handled yourself very well today."

Tom smiled back, still processing what had happened. "Thank you, Ms. Parker. I was so nervous, but I'm glad it all worked out."

As he left the office that day, Tom felt a newfound sense of confidence. He realized that facing his fears had not only helped him grow as a professional but also earned him the respect of his colleagues. Public speaking might still make him nervous, but now he knew he could handle it.

Articulate - To express an idea or feeling clearly.

- Tom took a deep breath, trying to articulate his thoughts clearly.

Avoid - To keep away from or stop oneself from doing something.

- Tom usually tried to avoid public speaking whenever possible.

Colleague - A person with whom one works in a profession or business.

- The client and several of Tom's colleagues were already seated in the conference room.

Confident - Feeling or showing certainty about something.

- Ms. Parker was confident that Tom was the best person for the task.

Encourage - To give support, confidence, or hope to someone.

- Ms. Parker gave Tom an encouraging smile before he started the presentation.

Impress - To make someone feel admiration and respect.

- The client was impressed with Tom's presentation and expressed interest in working with him.

Intimidating - Making someone feel nervous or frightened.

- The conference room felt cold and intimidating to Tom as he prepared to present.

Nervous - Easily agitated or alarmed; feeling or showing anxiety.

- Tom was nervous about presenting in front of the client and his colleagues.

Potential - Having or showing the capacity to develop into something in the future.

- Tom was presenting their new marketing strategy to a potential client.

Strategy - A plan of action designed to achieve a long-term or overall aim.

- Tom's presentation focused on the new marketing strategy his team had developed.

3.

MEETING MADNESS

The clock on the wall showed 9:00 AM, and the team had just gathered in the conference room for their weekly meeting. There were eight people seated around the table, each with a notepad in front of them. Lisa, the project manager, was in charge of running the meeting, but as usual, there was no clear agenda.

"Alright, let's get started," Lisa said, flipping through her notes. "Does anyone have any updates on the Anderson project?"

A few team members exchanged confused glances. Nobody was sure who should speak first, and the room fell into an awkward silence. Finally, Mark, the software engineer, cleared his throat.

"Well, I've been working on the new features for the app," Mark began. "But I'm still waiting for the design team to finalize the layout."

The design team members, Anna and James, looked at each other. "We've been focused on another project," Anna admitted. "We didn't know you were waiting on us."

The discussion quickly turned into a debate about priorities. Everyone had something to say, but no one was listening. Voices overlapped, and the meeting became chaotic.

"Hold on, hold on," Lisa tried to regain control, but the conversation continued without any structure. It felt like everyone was talking in circles, and no decisions were being made. Time was slipping away, and the team still hadn't addressed half of the topics they needed to discuss.

By the time the meeting ended, everyone was frustrated. They had spent an hour talking, but nothing had been resolved. The Anderson project was still in limbo, and the team felt even more disorganized than before.

After the meeting, Lisa sat at her desk, thinking about what went wrong. She realized that the lack of an agenda had been a big mistake. Without a clear plan, the meeting had turned into a free-for-all, wasting everyone's time.

The next day, Lisa decided to change her approach. She spent some time drafting an agenda for the next meeting. She listed all the topics that needed to be discussed, assigned time slots for each one, and identified who should lead each discussion.

When the team gathered for their next meeting, they noticed the difference immediately. Lisa started by reviewing the agenda, making sure everyone was on the same page. As they moved through each topic, the discussion was focused and efficient. There was no more talking over each other, and decisions were made quickly.

By the end of the meeting, the team had made significant progress on the Anderson project, and everyone left the room feeling satisfied. They realized how much more they could accomplish with proper time management and a clear agenda.

"That was much better," Mark said as they walked out of the conference room. "We actually got things done today."

"Agreed," Anna added. "It's amazing how much easier it is when we know what we're supposed to talk about."

Lisa smiled, feeling a sense of accomplishment. The chaos of the previous meeting was now a thing of the past, and the team had learned an important lesson: with a clear agenda and effective time management, meetings could be productive and even enjoyable.

Agenda - A list of items to be discussed at a meeting.

- Lisa realized that the lack of an agenda had been a big mistake.

Debate - A formal discussion on a particular topic where opposing arguments are presented.

- The discussion quickly turned into a debate about priorities.

Efficient - Being effective without wasting time or effort.

- The discussion was focused and efficient during the next meeting.

Finalize - To complete or agree on the last details of something.

- Mark was waiting for the design team to finalize the layout.

Frustrated - Feeling annoyed or angry because of not being able to achieve something.

- By the time the meeting ended, everyone was frustrated.

Limbo - An uncertain situation that you cannot control and in which there is no progress or improvement.

- The Anderson project was still in limbo after the chaotic meeting.

Priorities - The things that are considered most important and need to be done first.

- The team members were debating about their priorities during the meeting.

Productive - Achieving a significant amount or result.

- With proper time management, meetings could be productive and enjoyable.

Regain - To get something back, especially an ability or quality, that you have lost.

- Lisa tried to regain control of the chaotic meeting.

Significant - Important or noticeable.

- By the end of the meeting, the team had made significant progress on the project.

4.

THE OFFICE GOSSIP

Emily was new to the office, having joined just a few months ago. She was eager to fit in and make friends with her colleagues. During lunch breaks, she often joined a group of coworkers who would chat about everything from weekend plans to the latest TV shows. However, the conversation often drifted toward gossip about other people in the office.

One day, as Emily was grabbing a cup of coffee in the break room, she overheard two of her colleagues, Rachel and Mike, talking in hushed tones. They were discussing a rumor they had heard about their manager, Mr. Davis. The rumor was that he was planning to leave the company soon because of disagreements with upper management.

"Can you believe it?" Rachel whispered. "If he leaves, things are going to get really messy around here."

"Yeah, I've heard the same thing," Mike replied. "But keep it quiet; we don't want this to get out."

Emily was surprised. Mr. Davis had always been professional and seemed happy with his job. She wondered if the rumor was true, but more importantly, she felt uneasy about how quickly the gossip was spreading. She decided not to say anything and returned to her desk, but the conversation lingered in her mind.

Over the next few days, Emily noticed that the atmosphere in the office had changed. People seemed more tense, and there were whispered conversations happening in every corner. The rumor about Mr. Davis had clearly spread, and it was affecting everyone's mood.

One afternoon, Mr. Davis called an all-staff meeting. He looked serious as he addressed the team. "I understand that there have been some rumors going around about me leaving the company," he began. "I want to set the record straight. I have no intention of leaving. These rumors are completely unfounded and are causing unnecessary stress in the office."

Emily felt a wave of guilt wash over her. She hadn't started the rumor, but she hadn't done anything to stop it either. Mr. Davis went on to talk about the importance of maintaining a professional and respectful environment at work.

"Gossip can be very damaging," he continued. "It creates mistrust and can ruin relationships. I encourage all of you to think carefully before spreading information that may not be true. Let's focus on our work and support each other."

After the meeting, Emily decided to approach Mr. Davis privately. She wanted to apologize for not speaking up sooner. "Mr. Davis, I'm sorry about the rumors," she said. "I didn't start them, but I also didn't try to stop them, and I realize now how harmful that was."

Mr. Davis smiled kindly. "Thank you for saying that, Emily. It takes courage to admit when we've made a mistake. Just remember that in the future, if you hear something that doesn't sound right, it's best to go directly to the source rather than let it spread."

From that day on, Emily made a conscious effort to avoid participating in office gossip. She focused on her work and encouraged her colleagues to do the same. The atmosphere in the office gradually improved, and the team became more united.

Emily learned a valuable lesson about the power of words and the importance of confidentiality in the workplace. She realized that it was better to address issues directly and professionally, rather than contribute to an environment of gossip and speculation.

Colleague - A person you work with, especially in a professional or business environment.
- Emily wanted to make friends with her colleagues in the office.

Rumor - A piece of information or a story that is passed from person to person but has not been proven to be true.
- The rumor about Mr. Davis leaving the company spread quickly.

Gossip - Casual or unconstrained conversation or reports about other people, typically involving details that are not confirmed as true.
- Emily decided to avoid participating in office gossip.

Confidentiality - The state of keeping information secret or private.
- Emily learned the importance of confidentiality in the workplace.

Tense - Feeling or showing nervousness or anxiety.
- The atmosphere in the office became tense after the rumor spread.

Unfounded - Having no basis in fact; not supported by evidence.
- Mr. Davis said that the rumors were completely unfounded.

Professional - Relating to or connected with a profession or job.
- Mr. Davis emphasized the importance of maintaining a professional environment.

Mistrust - Lack of trust or confidence.
- Gossip creates mistrust and can ruin relationships.

Address - To speak to a group of people, especially to make an official announcement.

- Mr. Davis called a meeting to address the rumors.

Speculation - The forming of a theory or conjecture without firm evidence.

- Emily realized that contributing to speculation was harmful.

5.

CUSTOMER COMPLAINTS

Jane had always considered herself a patient person, but today was really testing her limits. She worked at a popular electronics store, and it seemed like every difficult customer in town had decided to visit her store that morning.

The first customer of the day, Mr. Thompson, was upset about a faulty television. "This TV stopped working after just two weeks! I demand a refund!" he shouted, waving his receipt in the air. Jane stayed calm and smiled.

"Let me take a look at that for you, Mr. Thompson," she said. "I'm really sorry about the inconvenience. We can either replace the television for you or offer a refund, whichever you prefer."

Mr. Thompson hesitated for a moment, then sighed. "I guess a replacement would be fine."

Jane quickly processed the exchange and apologized once more for the trouble. As Mr. Thompson left the store with his new TV, Jane felt relieved. But her relief was short-lived.

The next customer, Mrs. Garcia, was unhappy about a phone she had purchased. "This phone's battery doesn't last more than a few hours," she complained. "I've been trying to reach your customer service for days, but no one answers!"

Jane nodded sympathetically. "I understand how frustrating that must be, Mrs. Garcia. Let's test the phone to see if there's a problem with the battery. If there is, we can replace it for you."

Mrs. Garcia crossed her arms and frowned, but she allowed Jane to check the phone. After running a few tests, Jane confirmed that the battery was defective. She apologized again and offered to replace the phone.

By the time Mrs. Garcia left, Jane was starting to feel the stress of dealing with so many complaints. But she knew she had to keep going. The next customer, Mr. Lee, approached her with a serious expression.

"I bought this laptop last month, and now it's not charging properly," he explained. "I need it for work, so this is a huge problem."

Jane could see the worry on his face. "I'm really sorry to hear that, Mr. Lee. Let's see if we can figure out what's wrong with the charger or the battery. If we can't fix it, we'll make sure you get a new laptop."

After a few minutes of troubleshooting, Jane discovered that the charger was indeed faulty. She replaced it with a new one and assured Mr. Lee that the laptop should work perfectly now. He thanked her and left the store, visibly relieved.

As the morning continued, Jane dealt with complaint after complaint. Each customer seemed more frustrated than the last, and Jane had to use all of her patience and problem-solving skills to keep them satisfied. By the time her lunch break arrived, she felt completely drained.

While eating her sandwich in the break room, Jane thought about how challenging the day had been. She realized that no matter how difficult the situation, staying calm and polite had helped her resolve every issue. She also understood that listening to customers and showing empathy were just as important as finding solutions to their problems.

When Jane returned to the sales floor, she felt more confident. She knew that the rest of the day would likely bring more complaints, but she was ready to handle them. After all, she had already proven to herself that she could stay professional and patient, no matter what.

Faulty - Not working properly; having defects.
- The customer was upset about the faulty television he had purchased.

Refund - Money that is returned to a customer who is not satisfied with a product or service.
- Mr. Thompson demanded a refund for his defective TV.

Inconvenience - Trouble or difficulty caused to one's personal comfort or requirements.
- Jane apologized for the inconvenience the faulty television had caused.

Replace - To put something new in the place of something old or damaged.
- Jane offered to replace the defective phone with a new one.

Defective - Having a fault or problem; not working correctly.
- The phone's battery was defective, so Jane offered a replacement.

Frustrating - Causing annoyance or anger because something is not going as expected.
- Mrs. Garcia found it frustrating that the phone's battery didn't last long.

Troubleshooting - The process of solving problems, especially with electronic devices.
- Jane spent time troubleshooting Mr. Lee's laptop issue.

Empathy - The ability to understand and share the feelings of another.

- Jane showed empathy by listening carefully to each customer's complaint.

Satisfy - To meet the expectations, needs, or desires of someone.

- Jane used her problem-solving skills to satisfy each frustrated customer.

Drained - Very tired or exhausted.

- By lunchtime, Jane felt completely drained from handling so many complaints.

6.

THE JOB INTERVIEW

Mark sat at his kitchen table, staring at his laptop screen. The email had arrived that morning: he had been invited for a job interview at a company he had always dreamed of working for. Excitement quickly turned into nerves as he realized how important this interview was. He had to make a great impression if he wanted to secure the position.

Mark knew he needed to prepare. The first thing he did was research the company. He read about their history, their products, and their mission statement. He wanted to show the interviewers that he was genuinely interested in the company, not just the job. As he took notes, he thought about how he could relate his own experience to what the company was looking for.

Next, Mark reviewed common interview questions. He practiced answering them in front of a mirror, trying to sound confident and natural. "Tell me about yourself," he said to his reflection, "Well, I have five years of experience in marketing, and I'm passionate about developing creative campaigns that drive results." He nodded, feeling a bit more confident.

One of the questions that worried Mark the most was, "What are your strengths and weaknesses?" He knew that answering this question well could make a big difference. He decided to focus on strengths that were relevant to the job. "I'm very detail-oriented," he practiced saying. "I make sure that every aspect of a campaign is perfect before it goes live." As for weaknesses, he thought it was important to be honest but strategic. "Sometimes, I can be too focused on details," he practiced. "But

I'm working on balancing the big picture with the finer details."

Mark also prepared questions to ask the interviewers. He knew that asking thoughtful questions would show that he was engaged and serious about the role. "What are the company's goals for the next five years?" he planned to ask. He also wanted to know more about the team he would be working with, so he prepared to ask, "Can you tell me more about the team's dynamic?"

On the day of the interview, Mark dressed in his best suit. He arrived at the office building 15 minutes early, as he knew punctuality was important. While waiting in the lobby, he took deep breaths to calm his nerves. He reminded himself that he had prepared well and that he just needed to stay focused.

When the interview began, Mark was greeted by a panel of three interviewers. They started with the usual questions, and Mark felt that his preparation was paying off. He answered confidently, making sure to highlight his relevant experience and skills. When they asked about his strengths and weaknesses, he delivered his practiced answers smoothly.

The interviewers then asked some unexpected questions. One of them asked, "How do you handle tight deadlines?" Mark hadn't specifically prepared for this question, but he stayed calm. "I prioritize tasks based on urgency and importance," he replied. "I'm also not afraid to ask for help if needed. I believe in working efficiently while maintaining quality."

At the end of the interview, Mark asked his prepared questions. The interviewers seemed impressed by his curiosity and understanding of the company's goals. They smiled and thanked him for his time.

As Mark left the office, he felt a sense of relief. The interview had gone well, and he was proud of how he had handled himself. Now, all he could do was wait for the result.

Over the next few days, Mark replayed the interview in his mind. He analyzed his answers, wondering if he could have said something differently. But he also reminded himself that he had done his best. A week later, he received a phone call from the company. The HR manager congratulated him—he had gotten the job!

Mark was thrilled. All his hard work and preparation had paid off. The experience taught him that being well-prepared and staying calm under pressure were key to succeeding in a job interview. He was excited to start his new role and prove that he was the right choice for the job.

Secure - To obtain or achieve something, especially after a lot of effort.
- Mark wanted to secure the job by making a great impression in the interview.

Impression - The effect or influence that something or someone has on a person's thoughts or feelings.
- Mark knew he had to make a strong impression during the interview.

Punctuality - The quality of being on time.
- Mark knew that punctuality was important, so he arrived 15 minutes early.

Dynamic - The way in which people or things interact or operate together.
- Mark was interested in learning about the team's dynamic.

Relevant - Closely connected or appropriate to what is being done or considered.
- Mark highlighted his relevant experience during the interview.

Panel - A group of people gathered to discuss or decide on something.

- Mark was interviewed by a panel of three people.

Urgency - The need for immediate action or attention.

- Mark prioritized tasks based on urgency and importance.

Efficiently - Performing or functioning in the best possible manner with the least waste of time and effort.

- Mark believed in working efficiently while maintaining quality.

Congratulate - To give someone good wishes for something they have achieved.

- The HR manager congratulated Mark on getting the job.

Experience - Knowledge or skill gained through involvement in or exposure to something.

- Mark's experience in marketing helped him during the interview.

7.

THE MISCOMMUNICATION

It was a typical Tuesday morning in the office, and everyone was busy with their tasks. Emma, the project manager, had just received an urgent request from a client. They needed a presentation ready by the end of the day, and it had to be flawless. Emma quickly gathered her team to discuss the project.

"Alright, everyone," Emma started, "we have a tight deadline. The client wants the presentation by 5 PM today. It's crucial that we all understand what needs to be done."

Emma assigned different parts of the presentation to each team member. Sarah was in charge of the design, John would handle the data analysis, and Mike was responsible for writing the content. Emma emphasized the importance of clear communication, knowing that even a small mistake could cause a delay.

As the team got to work, Emma sent an email to Mike with instructions for the content. She wrote, "Please include the latest sales figures and make sure the language is formal. Let me know if you need anything." But in her hurry, Emma made a critical mistake—she forgot to attach the document with the sales figures.

Mike received the email and started working on the content. He noticed that the figures were missing, but assumed Emma was too busy to send them. He decided to use the previous quarter's sales figures instead, thinking they would be close enough.

Meanwhile, Sarah was busy designing the slides. She had a specific idea in mind and wanted to discuss it with Emma. But when she tried to reach Emma, her phone was off. Frustrated, Sarah continued with her design, hoping Emma would approve it later.

John was working on the data analysis and realized that the sales figures he was using didn't match with what he had seen before. He sent a message to Mike, asking if he had received different data. Mike, still confident in his decision, replied that he was using the most recent data he had. John didn't question it further and continued his analysis.

By 4 PM, the presentation was almost complete. Emma finally checked her email and saw a message from Mike: "The content is ready, but I used last quarter's sales figures as the new ones weren't attached." Emma's heart sank. She had completely forgotten to send the updated figures to Mike, and now they were running out of time.

Panicked, Emma called a quick meeting. "We have a big problem," she said. "The sales figures in the presentation are outdated. We need to update them right away."

Mike looked surprised. "I thought the old figures would be fine," he said. "I didn't realize how important the new data was."

"It's my fault," Emma admitted. "I should have sent you the correct figures earlier. But we need to fix this now."

The team worked together to update the presentation. Sarah adjusted the design to fit the new figures, and John quickly reanalyzed the data. By 4:45 PM, they were done. Emma reviewed the presentation one last time, making sure everything was perfect.

At exactly 5 PM, Emma sent the presentation to the client. She sighed in relief, knowing that they had narrowly avoided a disaster. The client responded an hour later, praising the team for their excellent work.

Afterward, Emma gathered her team again. "I want to apologize for the mix-up earlier," she said. "This was a reminder of how important clear and precise communication is. We did a great job fixing the problem, but we could have avoided the stress if we had communicated better from the start."

The team nodded in agreement. They had learned a valuable lesson about the importance of clarity and double-checking information. From that day on, they made sure to communicate more effectively, ensuring that everyone was on the same page.

Urgent - Requiring immediate action or attention.

- Emma received an urgent request from a client that needed immediate attention.

Flawless - Without any mistakes; perfect.

- The client wanted the presentation to be flawless.

Deadline - The latest time or date by which something should be completed.

- The team had a tight deadline to complete the presentation by 5 PM.

Emphasize - To give special importance or prominence to something in speaking or writing.

- Emma emphasized the importance of clear communication to her team.

Assume - To suppose to be the case, without proof.

- Mike assumed that the previous quarter's sales figures would be close enough.

Approve - To officially agree to or accept as satisfactory.

- Sarah hoped Emma would approve her design later.

Panicked - To feel sudden uncontrollable fear or anxiety.

- Emma panicked when she realized the sales figures were outdated.

Outdated - No longer valid or useful; old-fashioned.

- The sales figures in the presentation were outdated.

Narrowly - By a small margin; barely.

- The team narrowly avoided a disaster by fixing the mistake in time.

Avoid - To keep away from or stop oneself from doing something.

- The team could have avoided the stress with better communication.

8.

THE PRODUCT LAUNCH

The conference room was buzzing with activity. It was two days before the highly anticipated product launch, and the team at Tech Innovations was working around the clock. The new smartphone, which was supposed to be the company's most exciting release yet, was almost ready, but there was still much to do.

Lisa, the project manager, called a meeting to review the final preparations. "Alright, team, we have just two days left," she said, glancing at the clock. "We need to ensure everything is perfect for the launch. Let's go over what needs to be done."

Tom, the marketing lead, reported on the promotional materials. "The ads are ready to go, but we're still waiting on a few graphics from the design team. We also need to finalize the social media posts."

Emma, from the design team, spoke up. "We've had some delays with the graphics because of a software glitch, but we're working on it. I expect we'll have everything by the end of today."

Meanwhile, Raj, the product engineer, was busy testing the final prototype. "We've encountered a minor issue with the battery life," he said. "It's not affecting performance, but we need to address it before the launch."

Lisa nodded. "Thanks for the update, Raj. It's crucial that we resolve any issues as quickly as possible. We can't afford any setbacks."

The team worked late into the night. Tom reviewed the marketing materials and adjusted the ads based on feedback. Emma and her team worked tirelessly to correct the graphics, ensuring they were high-quality and eye-catching. Raj and his team managed to fix the battery issue, but it took longer than they had hoped.

As the clock struck midnight, Lisa gathered the team once more. "We've made great progress, but we need to stay focused. Tomorrow is going to be a long day, and we need to make sure everything is in place for the launch event."

The next day, the team arrived at the venue early to set up for the launch event. They meticulously arranged the display stands, tested the presentation equipment, and prepared the demo units of the new smartphone. Despite their exhaustion, everyone was determined to make the launch a success.

By the time the guests started arriving, everything was ready. The product launch went off without a hitch. The attendees were impressed with the new smartphone, and the team's hard work paid off. Lisa felt a wave of relief and pride as she watched the event unfold.

After the event, the team celebrated their success. Lisa thanked everyone for their dedication and effort. "We did it! Our teamwork and determination made this launch a success. Great job, everyone!"

The team was exhausted but satisfied. They had faced numerous challenges, but their hard work and collaboration had led to a successful product launch. It was a reminder of the importance of teamwork, preparation, and perseverance.

Anticipated - Expected or looked forward to.

- The new smartphone was the company's most anticipated release yet.

Conference Room - A room where meetings are held.

- The team gathered in the conference room to discuss the product launch.

Promotional - Related to the activities of promoting a product.

- The marketing lead was working on the promotional materials for the launch.

Finalize - To complete or settle something.

- They needed to finalize the social media posts before the launch.

Glitch - A minor problem or malfunction.

- There was a software glitch that caused delays with the graphics.

Prototype - The first or preliminary version of a product.

- Raj was testing the final prototype of the smartphone.

Setback - A delay or problem that hinders progress.

- The team couldn't afford any setbacks with the product launch.

Meticulously - Done with great attention to detail.

- They meticulously arranged the display stands for the event.

Demo Units - Demonstration versions of a product used for display.

- The demo units of the new smartphone were prepared for the event.

Unfold - To develop or become clear over time.

- Lisa felt a wave of relief as she watched the event unfold.

9.

THE DIFFICULT CLIENT

Lucy sat at her desk, staring at her computer screen with a mixture of anxiety and determination. Today was the day she would have to handle a difficult client, Mr. Thompson, who had been causing trouble for weeks. He had a reputation for being demanding and critical, and Lucy had been dreading this meeting.

The clock struck 10:00 AM, and Mr. Thompson arrived promptly at the office. Lucy greeted him with a friendly smile, despite her nerves. "Good morning, Mr. Thompson. Thank you for coming in today. How can I assist you?"

Mr. Thompson wasted no time. "I'm very disappointed with the progress on our project. The last report was late, and the updates are not what I expected."

Lucy took a deep breath. "I'm sorry to hear that you're not satisfied. Let's discuss the issues you've encountered so we can address them. Can you please specify what concerns you have with the report?"

Mr. Thompson flipped through the documents he had brought with him. "The report was supposed to include detailed analysis and projections. Instead, it was just a summary with basic information. I need more thorough details to make informed decisions."

Lucy nodded, taking notes. "I understand. We've had some

delays, but I assure you we're working hard to resolve them. I'll ensure the next report includes all the necessary information and is delivered on time."

As the meeting continued, Lucy remained calm and professional, even when Mr. Thompson's demands seemed unreasonable. She listened carefully, acknowledged his concerns, and offered solutions. "We're also implementing a new review process to prevent any future issues. Will that work for you?"

Mr. Thompson seemed a bit more relaxed. "That sounds promising. I appreciate your willingness to improve things. Let's see how the next report turns out."

Lucy felt a wave of relief as the meeting came to an end. She had managed to keep her composure and address the client's concerns effectively. After Mr. Thompson left, she immediately set to work on the necessary adjustments.

Over the next few weeks, Lucy and her team put in extra effort to meet Mr. Thompson's expectations. They provided detailed reports and kept him updated on every step of the project. When the next meeting came around, Mr. Thompson was pleased with the progress. "I'm impressed with the improvements you've made. Keep up the good work."

Lucy was relieved and proud. She had learned that maintaining professionalism, listening carefully, and managing expectations were key to handling difficult clients. It wasn't always easy, but it was definitely worth the effort.

Demanding - Requiring a lot of effort or attention.
- Mr. Thompson had a reputation for being a demanding client.

Critical - Finding fault or judging harshly.

- The client's feedback was very critical of the report's content.

Dread - To feel anxious or fearful about something.

- Lucy had been dreading the meeting with Mr. Thompson.

Promptly - On time or without delay.

- Mr. Thompson arrived promptly at the office for his meeting.

Satisfy - To meet the needs or expectations of someone.

- Lucy worked hard to ensure the report satisfied Mr. Thompson's expectations.

Specify - To state or describe something clearly.

- Mr. Thompson asked Lucy to specify the details he wanted in the report.

Thorough - Detailed and complete.

- The report needed to include thorough analysis and projections.

Professionalism - The quality of being skilled and competent in a job.

- Lucy maintained her professionalism throughout the difficult meeting.

Composure - Calmness and self-control.

- Lucy managed to keep her composure despite Mr. Thompson's harsh criticism.

Implement - To put into effect or carry out.

- The team decided to implement a new review process to improve their work.

Adjustments - Changes or modifications made to improve something.

- Lucy and her team made adjustments based on Mr. Thompson's feedback.

Pleased - Feeling happy or satisfied.

- Mr. Thompson was pleased with the improvements in the project.

10.

THE FIRST DAY

John's heart raced as he approached the entrance of his new office building. It was his first day at the job, and he was both excited and nervous. He had spent weeks preparing for this role, but now that the day had arrived, he felt unsure about what to expect.

The receptionist greeted him with a warm smile. "Good morning! You must be John. Welcome to the team. I'm Sarah. Let me show you to your desk."

John followed Sarah down a corridor lined with framed awards and photographs of company events. They reached a modern open-plan office where several employees were already busy at their workstations.

"This will be your desk," Sarah said, pointing to a spot near the window. "Feel free to settle in and make yourself comfortable. I've left some materials on your desk to help you get started."

John thanked Sarah and took a seat. The desk was neatly arranged with a computer, a notepad, and a few office supplies. As he started to familiarize himself with his new surroundings, a colleague named Emily came over to introduce herself.

"Hi, I'm Emily. I've heard a lot about you. If you need any help or have questions about the office, just let me know," she said kindly.

John smiled, feeling a bit more at ease. "Thank you, Emily. I'm really looking forward to getting started. Is there anything I should know about the office culture or any tips for fitting in?"

Emily nodded. "Sure! One thing to remember is that we have regular team meetings every Monday morning. It's a good chance to catch up with everyone and discuss our progress. Also, don't be afraid to ask for help. Everyone here is very friendly and supportive."

As the day progressed, John attended an orientation session where he learned about the company's history, values, and procedures. He was introduced to his team members and given a tour of the office facilities, including the break room and the conference rooms.

By lunchtime, John felt overwhelmed but hopeful. He joined the team in the break room, where they chatted about weekend plans and shared some lighthearted stories. Although he was still adjusting to the new environment, he appreciated the warm welcome and the chance to start building relationships with his colleagues.

After lunch, John was assigned his first task: preparing a report for a client meeting. He focused on organizing the information and making sure everything was clear and accurate. With Emily's encouragement, he managed to complete the report and felt a sense of accomplishment.

As the end of the day approached, John reviewed his notes and packed up his belongings. He felt exhausted but excited about the opportunities that lay ahead. Despite the challenges of his first day, he was eager to return the next morning and continue learning and growing in his new role.

Race - To move quickly or with urgency.

- John's heart raced as he approached the entrance of his new office building.

Excited - Feeling very enthusiastic and eager.

- John was excited about starting his new job.

Nervous - Feeling anxious or worried.

- He was nervous about what to expect on his first day.

Receptionist - The person who greets visitors and handles administrative tasks at the front desk.

- The receptionist greeted John with a warm smile.

Warm - Friendly and kind.

- Sarah gave John a warm welcome to the team.

Corridor - A long passage in a building.

- Sarah led John down a corridor lined with framed awards.

Workstation - A designated area where an employee works.

- John's desk was located near the window in the open-plan office.

Familiarize - To become acquainted with something.

- John started to familiarize himself with his new surroundings.

Colleague - A person who works with someone in the same company or organization.

- Emily came over to introduce herself as a colleague.

Kindly - In a friendly and considerate manner.

- Emily spoke to John kindly, offering her help.

Culture - The shared values and behaviors of a group of people.

- Emily shared tips about the office culture with John.

Orientation - Introduction to a new job or organization, including basic information and procedures.

- John attended an orientation session to learn about the company's values.

Facilities - The buildings and equipment provided for a specific purpose.

- John was given a tour of the office facilities, including the break room.

Overwhelmed - Feeling unable to cope due to being overburdened.

- By lunchtime, John felt overwhelmed but hopeful.

Break room - A place where employees can relax and take breaks.

- John joined the team in the break room for lunch.

Task - A piece of work to be done.

- John was assigned the task of preparing a report.

Accurate - Correct and precise.

- He focused on making sure the report was clear and accurate.

Encouragement - Support or approval that inspires someone to do something.

- With Emily's encouragement, John managed to complete the report.

Accomplishment - A sense of achievement from completing something successfully.

- John felt a sense of accomplishment after finishing his report.

Exhausted - Extremely tired.

- John felt exhausted but excited at the end of his first day.

11.

THE OFFICE PARTY

The annual office party was one of the most anticipated events of the year at GreenTech Solutions. Employees looked forward to it not just for the food and drinks, but also for the chance to unwind and network in a more relaxed setting. This year, however, things didn't go as smoothly as planned.

As soon as Sarah arrived at the venue, she noticed that the decorations were a bit off. The balloons were mismatched, and the streamers were tangled. Despite these small issues, she tried to stay positive. After all, the party was supposed to be a time for fun and celebration.

Sarah's first stop was the drinks table, where she grabbed a glass of sparkling water. She noticed a few colleagues already mingling and chatting. She joined a group near the snack table, where she saw Tom from accounting and Lisa from marketing.

"Hi, everyone! How's it going?" Sarah asked with a friendly smile.

Tom was in the middle of telling a story about his weekend trip when Lisa interrupted with a loud laugh. Her laughter was a bit over the top and seemed to draw unwanted attention. Sarah could see some of their other colleagues glancing in their direction.

As the evening progressed, the situation at the party took a turn. A few guests had too much to drink and started behaving inappropriately. Some people were speaking loudly, and others were arguing in the corner. Sarah felt uncomfortable but tried to stay focused on enjoying herself.

Then, the music started playing too loudly, making conversation difficult. Sarah noticed that the event organizer, Mr. Stevens, was visibly stressed as he tried to manage the chaos. She felt sorry for him, knowing that organizing such an event could be challenging.

The highlight of the night was supposed to be the awards ceremony, where employees would be recognized for their hard work. However, due to the commotion, the ceremony was delayed. Sarah took the opportunity to speak with a few people she hadn't met before, making the most of the networking aspect of the party.

Despite the problems, Sarah managed to have some meaningful conversations and meet new people. She realized that while the party wasn't perfect, it was a good reminder of how important it is to handle unexpected situations with grace and professionalism. By the end of the night, she was grateful for the opportunity to connect with her colleagues and make new contacts.

As Sarah left the venue, she couldn't help but reflect on the night's events. She felt that the party had been a learning experience, teaching everyone the value of appropriate behavior and the importance of networking, even when things don't go as planned.

Anticipated - Expected or looked forward to with excitement.

- The annual office party was one of the most anticipated events of the year.

Unwind - To relax and relieve stress.

- Employees looked forward to the party as a chance to unwind.

Network - To interact with others to exchange information and develop professional connections.

- Sarah took the opportunity to network with people she hadn't met before.

Decorations - Items used to make a place look more festive or attractive.
- Sarah noticed that the decorations were a bit off.

Mismatched - Not matching or not in harmony.
- The balloons were mismatched, and the streamers were tangled.

Positive - Having a good attitude or outlook.
- Despite the issues, Sarah tried to stay positive.

Mingling - Socializing and interacting with others.
- She joined a group near the snack table, where she saw Tom and Lisa mingling.

Colleagues - People who work together in the same organization.
- Sarah noticed a few colleagues already mingling and chatting.

Interrupt - To stop someone from speaking or continuing.
- Lisa interrupted Tom with a loud laugh.

Unwanted - Not desired or wished for.
- Lisa's loud laughter seemed to draw unwanted attention.

Inappropriately - In a manner that is not suitable or proper.
- Some guests had too much to drink and started behaving inappropriately.

Commotion - A state of noisy confusion or disorder.
- Due to the commotion, the awards ceremony was delayed.

Organizer - A person who arranges or manages an event.

- Sarah noticed that the event organizer, Mr. Stevens, was visibly stressed.

Stressed - Feeling anxious or under pressure.

- Mr. Stevens was visibly stressed as he tried to manage the chaos.

Delayed - Postponed or held up.

- The ceremony was delayed due to the problems at the party.

Meaningful - Having significance or value.

- Sarah managed to have some meaningful conversations and meet new people.

Grateful - Feeling thankful or appreciative.

- By the end of the night, Sarah was grateful for the opportunity to connect with her colleagues.

Reflect - To think deeply or carefully about something.

- Sarah couldn't help but reflect on the night's events.

Learning experience - An event or activity from which one gains knowledge or insight.

- She felt that the party had been a learning experience.

Professionalism - The skill, good judgment, and polite behavior expected from someone in a work environment.

- The party was a good reminder of the importance of professionalism.

12.

THE ELEVATOR PITCH

Mike's heart raced as he stepped into the elevator on the top floor of the downtown office building. Today was a big day—he had a meeting with a potential investor who had a reputation for making quick decisions. Mike knew that he had only a few seconds to grab their attention with his business idea. This was his chance to make a lasting impression.

The elevator doors closed, and Mike found himself alone with the investor, Mr. Davis. He took a deep breath and started his pitch. "Hello, Mr. Davis," Mike said, trying to sound confident. "I'm Mike, and I'm here to introduce you to EcoMend, a revolutionary platform that connects environmentally conscious consumers with sustainable products."

Mr. Davis raised an eyebrow, signaling that he was listening but not yet fully convinced. Mike continued, "EcoMend makes it easy for users to find and purchase eco-friendly products by offering a curated selection from trusted brands. We use advanced algorithms to match products with individual preferences, ensuring that every purchase supports a greener planet."

Mike noticed Mr. Davis's eyes narrowing slightly, indicating curiosity. He pressed on, "Our platform also includes a unique feature where users can track their environmental impact and earn rewards for their sustainable choices. This not only encourages responsible shopping but also builds a loyal community of eco-conscious consumers."

As the elevator descended, Mike felt a mix of excitement and anxiety. He knew he had to keep his pitch brief and engaging.

"EcoMend is more than just a shopping platform," he said, "it's a movement towards a more sustainable future. We're currently seeking investment to expand our reach and enhance our technology."

The elevator dinged as they reached the lobby. Mr. Davis turned to Mike with a thoughtful expression. "I'm intrigued," he said. "Let's schedule a meeting to discuss this in more detail."

Mike felt a wave of relief and satisfaction. He had successfully delivered his elevator pitch and captured the investor's interest. As he walked away, he reflected on the importance of making every second count in such high-stakes situations. It wasn't just about having a great idea; it was about presenting it clearly and persuasively, even under pressure.

Investor - A person who puts money into a business or project with the hope of making a profit.

- Mike had a meeting with a potential investor, Mr. Davis.

Reputation - The beliefs or opinions that are generally held about someone or something.

- Mr. Davis had a reputation for making quick decisions.

Impression - An effect or influence that something or someone has on people.

- Mike had to make a lasting impression with his business idea.

Confident - Feeling sure of oneself or one's abilities.

- Mike tried to sound confident as he started his pitch.

Revolutionary - Involving a complete or dramatic change.

- EcoMend is a revolutionary platform that connects consumers with sustainable products.

Platform - A digital service or application where users interact or perform tasks.

- EcoMend is a platform that offers eco-friendly products.

Curated - Carefully selected and organized.

- The platform offers a curated selection from trusted brands.

Algorithms - A set of rules or processes for solving a problem.

- We use advanced algorithms to match products with individual preferences.

Preferences - A greater liking for one alternative over another.

- The algorithms match products with individual preferences.

Environmental impact - The effect that a company's actions have on the environment.

- Users can track their environmental impact and earn rewards.

Rewards - Benefits or prizes given for achieving something.

- Users earn rewards for their sustainable choices.

Encourages - Persuades or motivates someone to do something.

- The platform encourages responsible shopping.

Loyal - Showing firm and constant support or allegiance.

- The platform builds a loyal community of eco-conscious consumers.

Movement - A group of people working together for a shared goal.

- EcoMend is a movement towards a more sustainable future.

Expand - To increase in size, number, or importance.

- They were seeking investment to expand their reach.

Enhance - To improve the quality or value of something.

- The investment would help enhance their technology.

Persuasively - In a way that convinces others.

- Mike needed to present his idea clearly and persuasively.

High-stakes - Involving a lot of risk or the possibility of significant outcomes.

- Mike had to make a lasting impression in this high-stakes situation.

Satisfaction - The feeling of pleasure when something is achieved.

- Mike felt a wave of relief and satisfaction after his pitch.

Reflect - To think deeply or carefully about something.

- Mike reflected on the importance of making every second count.

13.

THE TEAM LEADER

Susan couldn't believe her ears when her manager, Mr. Thompson, told her she had been promoted to team leader. It was an exciting opportunity, but she knew it came with new responsibilities. She had always been a reliable team member, but leading a team was something entirely different.

On her first day as team leader, Susan felt a mix of excitement and nervousness. She had to address her new team and set the tone for how things would work going forward. As she walked into the meeting room, she took a deep breath and smiled. "Good morning, everyone," she began. "I'm Susan, and I'm thrilled to be your new team leader."

The team greeted her with a mix of curiosity and skepticism. Susan knew she had to earn their respect, not just by her words but by her actions. She started by listening to their concerns and suggestions, showing them that their opinions mattered. It was important for her to build trust and a positive working environment.

One of the first challenges Susan faced was delegation. She needed to assign tasks effectively and ensure that everyone was clear on their responsibilities. She held a team meeting to discuss the upcoming project and divided the work among her team members. "John, I'd like you to handle the data analysis. Lisa, you're in charge of coordinating with the clients. And Mark, please focus on the presentation slides."

Susan tried to make sure that each team member understood their role and had the resources they needed. She was determined to be supportive and approachable, but she also had to learn how to handle conflicts. When two team members disagreed about their tasks, Susan stepped in to mediate. "Let's find a solution that works for both of you," she suggested. "We need to collaborate to achieve our goals."

As the weeks went by, Susan noticed some improvements in the team's performance, but she also encountered difficulties. There were times when deadlines were missed, and misunderstandings occurred. Susan learned that leadership required patience and perseverance. She regularly checked in with her team to provide feedback and encourage them.

One day, the team faced a major issue when a crucial report was delayed. Susan had to act quickly to find a solution. She called an emergency meeting and gathered everyone to discuss the problem. "We need to come up with a plan to address this issue immediately," she said firmly. "Let's brainstorm ideas and see how we can fix this."

Susan's ability to stay calm under pressure and her commitment to solving problems helped the team recover from the setback. By the end of the project, the team had managed to meet their goals and deliver a successful outcome. Susan felt a sense of accomplishment and pride in her new role.

Reflecting on her journey, Susan realized that leadership was about more than just managing tasks; it was about inspiring and supporting her team. She knew that her role as a team leader would continue to evolve, and she was ready to face new challenges with confidence and determination.

Promoted - Given a higher position or rank within a company.

- Susan was promoted to team leader, which came with new responsibilities.

Responsibilities - Duties or tasks that one is required or expected to do.

- Leading a team came with new responsibilities for Susan.

Navigate - To manage or handle a situation or challenge.

- Susan had to navigate the challenges of leadership and delegation.

Delegation - The act of assigning tasks or responsibilities to others.

- One of Susan's challenges was effective delegation.

Address - To speak to a group or deal with an issue.

- Susan had to address her new team and set the tone for how things would work.

Curiosity - A strong desire to know or learn something.

- The team greeted Susan with a mix of curiosity and skepticism.

Skepticism - Doubt or uncertainty about something.

- Susan's new team greeted her with skepticism.

Respect - Admiration or regard for someone's abilities or qualities.

- Susan knew she had to earn the team's respect through her actions.

Trust - Confidence in the reliability or ability of someone or something.

- Building trust and a positive working environment was important for Susan.

Concerns - Worries or problems that need to be addressed.

- Susan listened to her team's concerns and suggestions.

Mediating - Attempting to resolve conflicts between parties.

- Susan had to mediate when two team members disagreed

about their tasks.

Collaborate - To work together with others to achieve a common goal.

- The team needed to collaborate to achieve their goals.

Perseverance - The quality of continuing to do something despite difficulties.

- Leadership required patience and perseverance from Susan.

Feedback - Information about performance or behavior used for improvement.

- Susan regularly checked in with her team to provide feedback.

Encourage - To give support, confidence, or hope to someone.

- Susan provided feedback and encouraged her team throughout the project.

Setback - An obstacle or problem that delays progress.

- The team faced a major setback when a crucial report was delayed.

Determine - To decide or conclude after consideration.

- Susan was determined to be supportive and approachable in her new role.

Mediate - To intervene in a dispute to help reach a resolution.

- Susan mediated the disagreement between two team members.

Brainstorm - To come up with ideas or solutions through discussion.

- Susan called an emergency meeting to brainstorm solutions for the report issue.

Accomplishment - A sense of achievement or success.

- Susan felt a sense of accomplishment after the successful outcome of the project.

14.

THE CONFERENCE CALL

Jenny was feeling confident as she prepared for the big conference call. Her team had been working hard on a new project, and this call was their chance to present their progress to the senior managers. She carefully reviewed her notes and checked the presentation slides, ensuring everything was perfect.

As the clock struck 10:00 AM, Jenny dialed into the conference call. She was the first one to join the virtual meeting room. "Good morning, everyone," she said cheerfully. "I hope you're all ready for our presentation."

Slowly, the other participants started to join the call. There was Lisa from the marketing department, Tom from the finance team, and Raj from IT. Each person had their own area of expertise, and Jenny was excited to showcase their collective work.

However, the call did not go as smoothly as Jenny had hoped. For starters, Tom's audio was cutting in and out. "Can you hear me?" Tom asked repeatedly, sounding frustrated. "I'm having trouble with my microphone."

Lisa was trying to share her screen, but the software kept freezing. "Sorry, it's not loading," she said, her voice tinged with stress. "I'm not sure what's going on."

Raj, who was supposed to troubleshoot the technical issues,

seemed overwhelmed. "I'm checking the settings," he said. "It might take a minute."

Jenny felt a knot of anxiety forming in her stomach. The presentation was already delayed, and it was clear that they were running out of time. She tried to keep the meeting on track. "Let's move on to the next topic while we sort out these issues," she suggested.

Despite Jenny's efforts, the call continued to be chaotic. At one point, Lisa accidentally muted herself while talking, and the team had to spend several minutes trying to figure out what she was saying. Raj was struggling to fix the screen-sharing problem, and Tom's microphone issues persisted.

Jenny knew that they needed a better plan for their next virtual meeting. She realized that preparation was key, and they needed to test all equipment and software before the call. She also understood the importance of clear communication and having a backup plan for technical problems.

After the meeting, Jenny gathered her team to discuss what went wrong. "We need to be more organized," she said. "Let's set up a checklist for our next call to make sure everything works smoothly."

The team agreed and decided to have a brief rehearsal before their next presentation. They also agreed to assign specific roles, so each person knew their responsibilities. Jenny felt more confident about the changes and was determined to make their next conference call a success.

Conference Call - A phone or video meeting with multiple participants.

> Jenny prepared thoroughly for the big conference call with the senior managers.

Confident - Feeling sure of oneself and one's abilities.

Jenny was feeling confident as she prepared for the conference call.

Presentation - A talk or display of information to an audience.

The call was their chance to present their progress on the project.

Participants - People who take part in an event or activity.

The participants included Lisa, Tom, and Raj.

Audio - Sound or the recording of sound.

Tom's audio was cutting in and out during the call.

Microphone - A device used to amplify or record sound.

Tom was having trouble with his microphone.

Freezing - When a computer program or application stops working.

Lisa's screen was freezing, preventing her from sharing.

Troubleshoot - To solve problems or fix issues with equipment.

Raj was trying to troubleshoot the technical issues.

Anxiety - A feeling of worry or nervousness.

Jenny felt a knot of anxiety forming in her stomach.

Chaotic - Extremely disorganized or confused.

The conference call continued to be chaotic due to technical issues.

Delayed - Made late or postponed.

The presentation was already delayed because of the problems.

Rehearsal - Practice or preparation for a performance or event.

The team decided to have a brief rehearsal before their next call.

Checklist - A list of items or tasks to be completed.

Jenny suggested creating a checklist to ensure everything was ready for the next call.

Organized - Arranged or planned in a systematic way.

The team needed to be more organized to avoid future problems.

Backup Plan - An alternative plan in case the main plan fails.

Jenny realized the importance of having a backup plan for technical problems.

Responsibilities - Duties or tasks that someone is expected to perform.

The team agreed to assign specific roles and responsibilities for the next meeting.

Tinged - Slightly affected or influenced by something.

Lisa's voice was tinged with stress as she struggled with the software.

Determine - To decide or make a conclusion about something.

Jenny was determined to make their next conference call a success.

Software - Programs and applications used on a computer.

The software Lisa was using for the presentation kept freezing.

Rehearsal - A practice session before a formal event or performance.

They planned a rehearsal to ensure the next conference call went smoothly.

15.

THE CONTRACT NEGOTIATION

David had always been confident in his role as a project manager, but today's task was different. He was about to enter a crucial contract negotiation with a new supplier, and he needed to get it right. His company had been eyeing a promising partnership that could significantly impact their next big project.

David arrived at the supplier's office with a mix of excitement and nervousness. He was met by Mr. Thompson, the supplier's representative, who greeted him with a firm handshake. "Welcome, David. I'm glad we could meet today," Mr. Thompson said.

"Thank you, Mr. Thompson. I'm looking forward to discussing our potential agreement," David replied, trying to sound as confident as possible.

The meeting began with Mr. Thompson presenting the supplier's offer. David listened carefully, taking notes on the terms and conditions. The offer seemed reasonable, but David knew there were areas that could be improved. He needed to ensure the deal was beneficial for both sides.

When Mr. Thompson finished, David took a deep breath and started his counteroffer. "I appreciate your proposal," he said. "However, there are a few points I'd like to discuss further. For instance, the delivery schedule seems a bit tight. We would need more flexibility on that."

Mr. Thompson raised an eyebrow but nodded. "I understand. What kind of schedule are you proposing?"

David outlined his suggested timeline and explained why it was necessary. "We need a bit more time to ensure everything is in place before the delivery. This will help us avoid any potential issues on our end."

The negotiation continued with back-and-forth discussions. David was careful to remain polite but firm. He used phrases like "I'd like to propose" and "Could we consider" to suggest changes while respecting Mr. Thompson's position.

After several hours of negotiation, they reached a compromise. The supplier agreed to extend the delivery schedule and adjust some of the payment terms. David felt a sense of relief and accomplishment. "I think we've come to a fair agreement," he said with a smile.

Mr. Thompson shook his hand again. "Agreed. I'm pleased with how we resolved this. We look forward to working with you."

As David left the office, he reflected on the day's events. Negotiations had tested his skills, but he had learned a lot about balancing assertiveness with diplomacy. He knew that successful negotiations required not only a good understanding of the contract details but also the ability to communicate effectively and find mutually beneficial solutions.

Negotiate - To discuss and agree on the terms of a deal or agreement.

- David had to negotiate a tricky contract with a new supplier.

Crucial - Extremely important or essential.

- Today's task was crucial for the success of the next big project.

Representative - A person who represents or acts on behalf of others.

- David was met by Mr. Thompson, the supplier's representative.

Proposal - A plan or suggestion put forward for consideration.

- Mr. Thompson presented the supplier's proposal.

Counteroffer - An offer made in response to another offer, usually with modifications.

- David made a counteroffer to address some of the terms in the original proposal.

Flexibility - The ability to adapt or adjust to changing circumstances.

- David requested more flexibility on the delivery schedule.

Timeline - A schedule of activities or events.

- David outlined his proposed timeline for the delivery.

Compromise - An agreement reached by each side making concessions.

- After hours of negotiation, they reached a compromise on the terms.

Assertiveness - The quality of being confident and forceful in a respectful manner.

- David needed to balance assertiveness with diplomacy during the negotiation.

Diplomacy - The art of dealing with people in a sensitive and effective way.

- Successful negotiations required good diplomacy and communication skills.

Terms - The conditions or requirements of an agreement or contract.

- They discussed the terms of the contract in detail.

Accomplishment - Something achieved successfully, often through effort.

- David felt a sense of accomplishment after reaching the agreement.

Discuss - To talk about something with others in order to reach a decision.

- They discussed the delivery schedule and payment terms during the meeting.

Suggest - To put forward an idea or plan for consideration.

- David used phrases like "I'd like to propose" to suggest changes.

Respect - To show consideration or regard for others' opinions or needs.

- David was careful to remain polite and show respect during the negotiation.

Communicate - To exchange information or ideas with others.

- Effective communication was key to finding a mutually beneficial solution.

Solution - An answer or resolution to a problem or challenge.

- They found a solution that worked for both parties involved.

Balance - To maintain stability between different elements or factors.

- David needed to balance his assertiveness with diplomacy during the talks.

Concession - Something given up or granted in order to reach an agreement.

- Both parties made concessions to finalize the contract.

Mutually Beneficial - Providing advantages or benefits to both parties involved.

- The goal of the negotiation was to reach a mutually beneficial agreement.

16.

THE OFFICE POLITICS

Rachel had always been known for her hard work and dedication. When she joined the marketing department at her new company, she was eager to make a good impression. However, she soon discovered that the office environment was more complicated than she had anticipated.

One morning, Rachel overheard two of her colleagues, Sarah and Tom, discussing their upcoming project. They were trying to figure out how to handle a difficult client. Rachel was new and didn't know much about the client yet, but she wanted to help. She approached them and offered her assistance.

"Hey, I heard you talking about the client. If you need any help, I'd be happy to pitch in," Rachel said with a friendly smile.

Sarah glanced at Tom and then at Rachel. "That's very kind of you, Rachel. But, um, we've got it covered for now. Thanks anyway."

Rachel felt a bit awkward but didn't let it discourage her. She knew that establishing good relationships at work was important, but she also wanted to avoid stepping on anyone's toes.

Later that week, Rachel was invited to a team meeting where they discussed the project strategy. During the meeting, she noticed that Sarah and Tom were very close to their manager, Alex. They seemed to have a lot of influence and were always quick to agree with his ideas. Rachel wondered if this was a sign of office politics.

As the days went by, Rachel saw that office politics was a real issue. Some colleagues were trying to outshine each other, while others were just trying to stay under the radar. Rachel found herself caught in the middle. She didn't want to get involved in the back-and-forth of office politics, but she also didn't want to be left out or seem uncooperative.

One afternoon, Rachel's manager, Alex, asked her to prepare a report for an important client presentation. Rachel was excited but also nervous. She knew this was a big opportunity to showcase her skills. However, she also noticed that Sarah and Tom were working on a similar report and had been discussing it in detail with Alex.

Rachel decided to approach Alex and discuss her report. "Alex, I've been working on the client presentation report, and I wanted to make sure it aligns with what Sarah and Tom are doing. Can we go over it together?"

Alex was pleased with Rachel's initiative. "Sure, Rachel. Let's review it and see how it fits with the overall strategy."

After the review, Alex gave Rachel some feedback and encouraged her to continue working on the report. Rachel felt relieved and confident that she was on the right track.

The presentation day arrived, and Rachel's report was well-received by the client. Her professionalism and preparation paid off. Rachel also noticed that her colleagues were supportive and congratulated her on the successful presentation.

Rachel had learned an important lesson about office politics. She realized that while it was essential to maintain positive relationships with her colleagues, staying true to her values and focusing on her work was even more important. By being proactive and communicating openly, Rachel managed to navigate the office politics and prove her worth without getting involved in unnecessary drama.

Influence - The ability to affect or change someone or something.

> Sarah and Tom had a lot of influence over their manager, Alex.

Colleague - A person who works with someone in a professional setting.

> Rachel offered her assistance to her colleagues, Sarah and Tom.

Discourage - To cause someone to lose confidence or enthusiasm.

> Rachel felt a bit awkward but didn't let it discourage her.

Establish - To set up or create something.

> Rachel knew that establishing good relationships at work was important.

Back-and-forth - Repeated exchange of comments or actions between two or more people.

> Rachel found herself caught in the back-and-forth of office politics.

Under the Radar - To avoid attracting attention or being noticed.

> Some colleagues were trying to stay under the radar.

Initiative - The ability to assess and initiate things independently.

> Rachel decided to take the initiative and discuss her report with Alex.

Align - To bring into agreement or cooperation.

> Rachel wanted to make sure her report aligned with what Sarah and Tom were doing.

Professionalism - The competence or skill expected of a professional.

Rachel's professionalism and preparation paid off during the presentation.

Proactive - Taking action to make changes or address issues before they become problems.

By being proactive and communicating openly, Rachel navigated office politics effectively.

Presentation - A formal introduction or display of information.

Rachel prepared a report for an important client presentation.

Opportunity - A chance to do something or achieve something.

Rachel saw the report as a big opportunity to showcase her skills.

Relieved - Feeling reassured and less anxious.

Rachel felt relieved after receiving feedback and encouragement from Alex.

Supportive - Providing encouragement or help.

Rachel's colleagues were supportive and congratulated her on the successful presentation.

Drama - Excitement or conflict in a situation, often involving unnecessary complications.

Rachel managed to prove her worth without getting involved in unnecessary office drama.

17.

THE DRESS CODE

Emma had just started her new job at a prestigious marketing firm. She was excited but also a bit nervous about fitting in. On her first day, she wanted to make a good impression. She had heard that the company had a dress code, but she wasn't sure what it was.

Emma decided to wear a smart, professional outfit—an elegant blouse and a pair of tailored trousers. She felt confident as she walked into the office, ready to tackle her new responsibilities.

As soon as she arrived, she noticed that most of her colleagues were dressed in very casual attire. Some wore jeans and t-shirts, while others had on shorts and sneakers. Emma began to feel uneasy. She had thought that the office dress code required more formal clothing.

When Emma's manager, Mr. Thompson, walked by, he gave her a warm smile. "Good morning, Emma. You look very professional today."

"Thank you, Mr. Thompson," Emma replied, feeling a bit self-conscious.

Throughout the morning, Emma noticed several curious glances from her coworkers. She overheard some of them whispering about the "new girl" who was dressed too formally. Emma tried to ignore the comments and focus on her work, but the situation made her uncomfortable.

By lunchtime, Emma's colleague, Lisa, approached her. "Hey, Emma. I couldn't help but notice your outfit. It's really nice, but most of us wear casual clothes here. Did you not get the memo about the dress code?"

Emma was surprised. "Oh, I didn't know. I thought the dress code was more formal."

Lisa smiled reassuringly. "No worries! It's usually pretty relaxed. Next time, you can dress down a bit. But I must say, you look great!"

Emma appreciated Lisa's friendly advice and decided to adjust her wardrobe accordingly. That afternoon, she asked Mr. Thompson about the office dress code to avoid any further misunderstandings.

Mr. Thompson explained, "Our dress code is quite flexible. We want everyone to feel comfortable, but we also appreciate when people dress neatly and professionally. It's about finding the right balance."

Emma felt relieved to get clarity on the matter. She realized that while it was important to adhere to the dress code, it was also crucial to adapt and feel comfortable in her own style. The next day, Emma chose a more casual outfit that still looked neat and presentable.

Her colleagues noticed the change and complimented her on her new look. Emma felt more at ease and confident, knowing she had adjusted to the office culture.

By the end of the week, Emma had settled in comfortably, and she was grateful for the friendly guidance she received. She learned an important lesson about the importance of understanding and adapting to workplace norms while maintaining her own sense of professionalism.

Prestigious - Having high status and respect.
- Emma was excited to start her job at the prestigious

marketing firm.

Elegant - Graceful and stylish in appearance or manner.
- She wore an elegant blouse and a pair of tailored trousers.

Tailored - Made to fit well; customized.
- Emma's tailored trousers made her look professional.

Casual - Relaxed and informal.
- Most of her colleagues were dressed in casual attire.

Uneasy - Feeling uncomfortable or worried.
- Emma began to feel uneasy when she noticed her colleagues' casual dress.

Self-conscious - Feeling awkward or embarrassed about oneself.
- She felt a bit self-conscious when Mr. Thompson complimented her outfit.

Memo - A written message used for communication within an organization.
- Emma hadn't received the memo about the dress code.

Reassuringly - In a way that makes someone feel less worried.
- Lisa smiled reassuringly and explained the casual dress code.

Flexible - Able to adapt to different conditions.
- The dress code at the office was quite flexible.

Balance - A state of equilibrium or equal distribution.
- It's about finding the right balance between comfort and professionalism.

Comfortable - Feeling relaxed and free from worry.
- Emma felt more comfortable in her new, casual outfit.

Adjust - To change something to make it better or more suitable.

- Emma decided to adjust her wardrobe accordingly.

Guidance - Advice or information aimed at helping someone.

- Emma was grateful for the friendly guidance she received.

Norms - Accepted standards or practices.

- Emma learned about adapting to workplace norms.

Professionalism - The competence or skill expected of a professional.

- Emma maintained her professionalism while adjusting to the casual dress code.

18.

THE PROMOTION

Jenny had been working at her company for several years. She enjoyed her job and felt she had grown a lot since she first started. Recently, she learned about a potential promotion to a senior position. This was an opportunity she had been hoping for, and she knew it would require hard work and dedication.

Determined to earn the promotion, Jenny set clear goals for herself. She started by reviewing her job performance and identifying areas where she could improve. She realized that while she was good at her current tasks, she needed to develop new skills to be considered for the senior role.

Jenny began by taking online courses related to project management and leadership. She also sought feedback from her colleagues and supervisors to understand her strengths and areas for growth. With every piece of advice, Jenny worked diligently to enhance her skills.

In addition to her professional development, Jenny knew that self-advocacy was crucial. She started by keeping a record of her accomplishments and contributions to the team. She wanted to ensure that her efforts did not go unnoticed.

One day, Jenny's manager, Mr. Carter, called her into his office. Jenny felt a mix of excitement and nervousness as she walked in. Mr. Carter congratulated her on her hard work and dedication. He acknowledged the improvements she had made and praised her for taking initiative.

"Jenny," Mr. Carter said, "I've noticed your dedication and the progress you've made. It's clear that you've put in a lot of effort to develop your skills. I believe you're ready for the promotion."

Jenny's heart raced with joy. She thanked Mr. Carter for the opportunity and assured him that she would continue to work hard in her new role. She felt proud of her achievements and grateful for the support she received from her colleagues.

As she started her new position, Jenny faced new challenges and responsibilities. She had to manage larger projects and lead a team. It wasn't always easy, but she approached each challenge with the same dedication she had shown before.

Jenny's journey taught her the importance of perseverance, skill development, and advocating for oneself. She realized that with commitment and hard work, she could achieve her career goals and grow professionally.

Dedication - Commitment to a task or purpose.
- Jenny's dedication to her work helped her earn the promotion.

Determine - To decide firmly on a course of action.
- Jenny was determined to earn the promotion by working hard.

Accomplishments - Achievements or successes.
- She kept a record of her accomplishments to show her progress.

Initiative - The ability to take action independently.
- Jenny took the initiative to improve her skills through online courses.

Feedback - Information or criticism about one's performance.
- She sought feedback from her colleagues to understand her strengths.

Enhance - To improve or increase.

- Jenny worked diligently to enhance her skills for the senior role.

Advocacy - Support or promotion of a cause or idea.

- Self-advocacy was crucial for Jenny to ensure her efforts were recognized.

Performance - How well someone does a job or task.

- Jenny reviewed her job performance to identify areas for improvement.

Leadership - The ability to guide or manage a group.

- Jenny took courses related to leadership to prepare for her new role.

Responsibilities - Duties or tasks that one is required to do.

- Jenny faced new responsibilities in her senior position.

Perseverance - Continued effort to do or achieve something despite difficulties.

- Jenny's perseverance helped her overcome challenges in her new role.

Opportunities - Chances or possibilities to do something.

- The promotion was an opportunity Jenny had been hoping for.

Contribution - An act of giving or adding something.

- Her contributions to the team were acknowledged during the promotion review.

Commitment - A pledge or firm dedication to a cause.

- Jenny's commitment to her work was evident in her efforts.

Accomplishments - Achievements or things done successfully.

- She listed her accomplishments to highlight her readiness for promotion.

19.

THE NETWORKING EVENT

Tim had always heard about the importance of networking, but he never fully understood it until he was invited to his first networking event. It was an evening event at a downtown hotel, and Tim felt a mix of excitement and nervousness as he prepared to attend.

When Tim arrived at the venue, he was greeted by a friendly host who handed him a name tag and directed him to the main hall. The room was filled with professionals from various industries, all engaged in animated conversations. Tim noticed that everyone seemed to know how to mingle effortlessly, and he felt a bit out of place.

Determined to make the most of the event, Tim took a deep breath and approached a small group discussing a recent industry trend. He introduced himself, saying, "Hi, I'm Tim. I'm new to the field and eager to learn more about the latest developments."

The group welcomed him warmly and began sharing their insights. Tim listened attentively, nodding and asking questions. He made sure to remember names and details about each person he spoke with, knowing this would help him build connections.

Throughout the evening, Tim practiced engaging in small talk, which involved discussing topics like recent projects, industry news, and mutual interests. He found that being genuinely curious and asking open-ended questions helped keep the conversations flowing.

At the end of the event, Tim felt more confident. He had collected several business cards and had meaningful conversations with a few key individuals. As he left the hotel, he reflected on the importance of following up. Tim made a note to send personalized thank-you emails to those he met, reminding them of their conversation and expressing his interest in staying in touch.

Tim's experience at the networking event taught him that building professional relationships is not just about collecting contacts but also about creating genuine connections and maintaining them over time.

Networking - The action or process of interacting with others to exchange information and develop professional relationships.

- Attending the networking event helped Tim understand the value of making new professional connections.

Venue - The place where an event or meeting takes place.

- The networking event was held at a downtown hotel venue.

Greeting - A polite word or sign of welcome or recognition.

- Tim received a warm greeting from the host as he arrived at the event.

Mingle - To move around and socialize at a gathering or event.

- Tim felt a bit out of place at first but soon learned to mingle with other attendees.

Animated - Lively and full of energy.

- The room was filled with animated conversations and discussions.

Effortlessly - With ease and without difficulty.
- Everyone at the event seemed to mingle effortlessly.

Introduce - To present someone to others by name.
- Tim introduced himself to the group with a friendly greeting.

Insights - Valuable or useful ideas or understanding about a subject.
- The group shared their insights on recent industry trends with Tim.

Attentively - Paying close attention.
- Tim listened attentively to the discussions to learn more.

Small Talk - Casual conversation about trivial matters.
- Tim practiced engaging in small talk to keep conversations flowing.

Genuinely - Sincerely and without pretense.
- Being genuinely curious about others helped Tim build connections.

Open-ended Questions - Questions that cannot be answered with a simple "yes" or "no" and encourage a detailed response.
- Tim asked open-ended questions to keep the conversation interesting.

Collect - To gather or accumulate.
- Tim collected several business cards from the people he met.

Personalized - Made to suit a particular person.
- Tim planned to send personalized thank-you emails to those he met at the event.

Follow Up - To take additional actions after an initial contact or event.

- Following up with personalized emails helped Tim maintain the connections he made.

Meaningful - Having significance or value.

- Tim had meaningful conversations with a few key individuals at the event.

Reflect - To think deeply or carefully about something.

- Tim reflected on his experience as he left the hotel.

20.

THE TIGHT DEADLINE

The marketing team at GreenTech Innovations had always prided themselves on their ability to deliver high-quality campaigns. But this time, they were facing a real challenge. Their latest project had a tight deadline, and the pressure was on.

Sarah, the project manager, called a team meeting early Monday morning to discuss the plan. "We need to finish the campaign by Friday," she said, looking at her team with determination. "That gives us just five days. We'll need to work efficiently and stay focused."

The team groaned a bit at the news but knew that this was part of the job. Alex, the creative director, suggested, "Let's break down the tasks and assign each one to a team member. This way, we can manage our time better."

Sarah agreed, and they started organizing the workload. They made a list of all the tasks that needed to be completed, from designing the graphics to writing the content and reviewing everything. Each task was assigned a specific deadline to ensure they stayed on track.

As the days went by, the team worked tirelessly. There were late nights and a few stressful moments, but everyone was committed to meeting the deadline. They held brief daily meetings to discuss their progress and tackle any problems that came up.

On Wednesday, they faced a setback when one of the key graphic designers fell ill. Sarah quickly rearranged the tasks and asked the team to help out. Despite the added pressure, they managed to adjust their plans and keep moving forward.

By Friday afternoon, the campaign was almost complete. The team worked together to make the final adjustments and ensure everything was perfect. They submitted the campaign just before the deadline, exhausted but proud of their hard work.

Sarah congratulated the team. "Great job, everyone! We made it through a tough week and delivered an excellent campaign on time. This experience showed us the importance of teamwork and managing our time effectively."

The tight deadline had tested their ability to work under pressure, but in the end, it strengthened their skills and brought them closer together as a team.

Deadline - The latest time or date by which something should be completed.
- The team had a tight deadline to complete the marketing campaign.

Pressure - The stress or urgency to achieve something.
- The pressure was high as the team faced the tight deadline.

Efficiently - In a way that achieves maximum productivity with minimum wasted effort.
- To meet the deadline, the team needed to work efficiently.

Focused - Paying close attention and not being distracted.
- Everyone needed to stay focused to complete their tasks on time.

Groan - To make a low sound of discomfort or displeasure.
- The team groaned when they heard about the tight deadline.

Creative Director - The person in charge of the creative aspects of a project.

- Alex, the creative director, suggested breaking down the tasks.

Organizing - Arranging or structuring tasks or items systematically.

- They spent the morning organizing the workload into manageable tasks.

Workload - The amount of work to be done.

- The team had a heavy workload to complete before the deadline.

Setback - An obstacle or problem that delays progress.

- The team faced a setback when one of the designers fell ill.

Rearrange - To change the order or arrangement of something.

- Sarah quickly rearranged the tasks to address the setback.

Commitment - The state of being dedicated to a task or purpose.

- The team showed great commitment to meeting the deadline.

Adjust - To make small changes to something to improve it or make it work better.

- They adjusted their plans to accommodate the unexpected problem.

Exhausted - Very tired or worn out.

- The team was exhausted but satisfied after submitting the campaign.

Congratulate - To praise someone for their achievement.

- Sarah congratulated the team on their hard work and success.

Strengthen - To make something stronger or more effective.

- The tight deadline helped strengthen the team's skills and unity.

Experience - The process of doing and seeing things and having them happen to you.

- The experience of working under pressure taught the team valuable lessons.

Submit - To present or hand in something for review or approval.

- They submitted the campaign just before the deadline.

Adjustments - Small changes made to improve or correct something.

- The team made final adjustments to ensure the campaign was perfect.

Tackle - To deal with or handle something.

- They tackled any problems that arose during their daily meetings.

Commitment - The quality of being dedicated to a cause or activity.

- The team's commitment was evident in their hard work and dedication.

21.

THE CLIENT PRESENTATION

Laura was excited but nervous about her upcoming client presentation. She had spent weeks preparing for this important meeting with Tech Solutions, one of their biggest clients. The presentation was crucial because it could lead to a significant contract for her company.

Laura started her preparation by researching Tech Solutions thoroughly. She learned about their needs, recent projects, and the challenges they faced. This information helped her understand the client's perspective and tailor her presentation to address their specific concerns.

Early on the day of the presentation, Laura set up the meeting room. She arranged the seating so that everyone would be comfortable and positioned the projector for the best view. Laura made sure her slides were clear and well-organized, with key points highlighted. She practiced her speech several times to ensure she could deliver it smoothly and confidently.

When the meeting began, Laura introduced herself and welcomed the clients. She started the presentation by briefly summarizing their company's history and achievements. Laura then moved on to explain how their proposed solution would benefit Tech Solutions. She used simple language and clear visuals to make her points easy to understand.

Throughout the presentation, Laura paid close attention to the clients' reactions. She noticed a few puzzled looks and quickly adjusted her explanations to clarify any confusion. Laura also encouraged questions, which helped engage the clients and show that she was open to feedback.

At the end of the presentation, Laura summarized the main points and provided a clear call to action. She thanked the clients for their time and asked if they had any additional questions or needed further information. The clients seemed impressed and appreciative of Laura's thorough preparation and clear communication.

After the meeting, Laura felt relieved and proud of her performance. She realized that understanding the audience and delivering a well-prepared message were key to a successful presentation. Her hard work and attention to detail had paid off, and she was optimistic about the potential contract.

Presentation - A talk or demonstration given to an audience, often using slides or visual aids.

- Laura spent weeks preparing her presentation for the client meeting.

Crucial - Extremely important or essential.

- The presentation was crucial for securing a significant contract.

Tailor - To adjust or modify something to suit a particular purpose or audience.

- Laura tailored her presentation to address the client's specific concerns.

Perspective - A particular way of thinking about something or a point of view.

- Understanding the client's perspective helped Laura prepare more effectively.

Setup - The arrangement or organization of something.

- Laura set up the meeting room to ensure everything was in order.

Projector - A device used to display images or presentations onto a screen.

- Laura positioned the projector for the best view of her slides.

Organized - Arranged or structured in a clear and systematic way.

- She made sure her slides were well-organized with key points highlighted.

Confidently - In a way that shows self-assurance or certainty.

- Laura practiced her speech to deliver it confidently during the presentation.

Introduce - To present someone or something for the first time.

- Laura introduced herself at the beginning of the meeting.

Summarize - To give a brief statement of the main points.

- Laura summarized the main points of her presentation at the end.

Beneficial - Providing an advantage or improvement.

- Laura explained how their proposed solution would benefit the client.

Visuals - Images, graphs, or other visual elements used to support a presentation.

- She used clear visuals to make her points easier to understand.

Engage - To attract or hold the attention of someone.

- Encouraging questions helped engage the clients during the presentation.

Feedback - Information or reactions about something that can be used for improvement.

- Laura was open to feedback from the clients.

Relieved - Feeling relaxed and free from worry after a stressful situation.

- Laura felt relieved after the presentation was over.

Optimistic - Having a positive outlook or hope for the future.

- Laura was optimistic about the potential contract following her successful presentation.

Address - To deal with or speak about a particular issue or topic.

- Laura addressed the client's specific concerns in her presentation.

Adjust - To change something slightly to improve it.

- She adjusted her explanations to clarify any confusion.

Clarify - To make something clear or easier to understand.

- Laura clarified any confusion by adjusting her explanations.

Appreciative - Feeling or showing gratitude or thankfulness.

- The clients were appreciative of Laura's thorough preparation.

22.

THE PROPOSAL

James had just been assigned one of the most critical tasks in his career: writing a business proposal for a major client. The proposal was crucial because it would determine whether their company could secure a significant contract. James knew that to win the client's favor, he needed to write a compelling and detailed proposal.

He began by gathering all the necessary information. James carefully reviewed the client's needs and the goals they wanted to achieve. He also looked at previous proposals that his company had written to see what had worked well and what could be improved. This research helped him understand what the client was looking for and how to present his ideas effectively.

James started drafting the proposal by outlining the key sections: an introduction, a description of the services offered, the benefits to the client, and the terms of the contract. He made sure each section was clear and persuasive. He knew that using strong, convincing language was essential to make the proposal stand out.

As he wrote, James paid close attention to detail. He made sure the proposal was free of errors and that all the information was accurate. He included specific examples of how their services had benefited other clients, which added credibility to his proposal. James also used visuals, such as charts and graphs, to make complex information easier to understand.

After completing the first draft, James reviewed the proposal several times. He asked his colleagues for feedback and made revisions based on their suggestions. He wanted to ensure that the proposal was not only professional but also engaging. James knew that a well-prepared proposal could make a significant difference in winning the contract.

On the day of the presentation, James felt confident. He had put in the effort to create a proposal that was both persuasive and detailed. During the meeting with the client, James presented the proposal clearly and answered all their questions. The client seemed impressed with the thoroughness and clarity of the proposal.

In the end, James's hard work paid off. The company won the contract, and James received praise for his exceptional proposal. He realized that writing a successful proposal required a combination of persuasive language, attention to detail, and a deep understanding of the client's needs.

Proposal - A formal plan or suggestion, usually presented in writing, for consideration.

- James worked hard on the proposal to secure the contract.

Crucial - Extremely important or necessary.

- Writing the proposal was a crucial task for James's career.

Compelling - Capable of attracting attention or interest.

- He needed to write a compelling proposal to win the client's favor.

Detail - A small or minor feature of something.

- James paid close attention to detail to ensure the proposal was accurate.

Effective - Producing a desired result or outcome.

- The research helped him understand how to present his

ideas effectively.

Drafting - Creating a preliminary version of a document.

- James started drafting the proposal by outlining the key sections.

Persuasive - Capable of convincing someone to believe or do something.

- Using persuasive language was essential to make the proposal stand out.

Credibility - The quality of being trusted or believed in.

- Including specific examples added credibility to James's proposal.

Visuals - Images, charts, or graphs used to illustrate or clarify information.

- James used visuals to make complex information easier to understand.

Revisions - Changes made to improve a document or work.

- He made revisions to the proposal based on his colleagues' feedback.

Engaging - Attracting and holding interest.

- James wanted the proposal to be both professional and engaging.

Presentation - The act of showing or explaining something to an audience.

- During the meeting, James presented the proposal clearly.

Feedback - Information or reactions about something that can be used for improvement.

- James asked his colleagues for feedback on the proposal.

Thoroughness - The quality of being detailed and careful.

- The client was impressed with the thoroughness of James's proposal.

Contract - A formal agreement between parties.

- The company won the contract thanks to James's exceptional proposal.

Client - A person or organization that uses the services of a professional person or company.

- James presented the proposal to the client in the meeting.

Example - A specific instance that illustrates a general principle or point.

- James included examples of how their services had benefited other clients.

Achievement - Something accomplished successfully, often requiring effort.

- Securing the contract was a significant achievement for James.

Outline - A general description or plan showing the essential features of something.

- He started by outlining the key sections of the proposal.

Accurate - Free from errors; correct.

- James made sure the proposal was accurate and free of errors.

23.

THE INTERNATIONAL MEETING

When the team at Global Solutions was informed about the upcoming meeting with international clients, everyone felt a mix of excitement and nervousness. This was an important opportunity to expand their business and build relationships across different cultures. The clients were coming from various countries, and the team needed to be well-prepared.

Rachel, the team leader, organized a briefing session to discuss the meeting. "We have clients from three different countries attending this meeting," she explained. "We need to understand their cultural backgrounds to communicate effectively and avoid misunderstandings."

To help with this, Rachel arranged a workshop on cross-cultural communication. The workshop focused on cultural differences, etiquette, and how to address clients respectfully. The team learned that different cultures had unique customs and expectations. For example, in some cultures, it was important to make small talk before discussing business, while in others, getting straight to the point was preferred.

James, a team member who had previously traveled abroad, shared his experiences. "In some countries, direct communication is valued, but in others, indirect communication is more common. It's crucial to adapt our approach based on who we are speaking to."

The day of the meeting arrived. The conference room was set up with refreshments, and the team was ready. The international clients entered, and the team greeted them warmly, using polite and formal language. They had prepared a presentation that was clear and easy to follow, with visuals to support their points.

During the meeting, Rachel noticed that the clients were taking notes and asking thoughtful questions. She made sure to listen actively and respond thoughtfully, recognizing that their questions were a sign of interest. The team members also made an effort to be aware of non-verbal cues, such as body language and facial expressions, which could indicate how the clients were reacting to their presentation.

As the meeting concluded, the clients expressed their appreciation for the team's effort to understand their cultural backgrounds and needs. They were impressed with the team's professionalism and the quality of the presentation. The meeting ended on a positive note, with agreements on the next steps and a plan for future collaboration.

Reflecting on the experience, Rachel felt proud of her team. They had successfully navigated the challenges of working with international clients and had learned valuable lessons about cross-cultural communication. The meeting had not only been a business success but had also strengthened their understanding of how to work effectively in a global environment.

International - Relating to or involving more than one country.

> The meeting with international clients taught the team about cultural differences.

Client - A person or organization that uses the services of a professional person or company.

> The clients were coming from various countries.

Opportunity - A situation or condition favorable for attainment of a goal.

> This was an important opportunity to expand their business.

Cultural - Relating to the ideas, customs, and social behavior of a society.

> Understanding their cultural backgrounds was crucial for effective communication.

Communication - The act of conveying information or ideas.

> The workshop focused on cross-cultural communication.

Etiquette - The customary code of polite behavior in society or among professionals.

> The team learned about the etiquette and how to address clients respectfully.

Customs - Traditional practices or behaviors specific to a culture.

> Different cultures have unique customs and expectations.

Direct - Straightforward and honest in manner.

> In some countries, direct communication is valued.

Indirect - Not straightforward or explicit; subtle.

> In other cultures, indirect communication is more common.

Adapt - To change or modify something to fit a new situation.

> It's crucial to adapt our approach based on who we are speaking to.

Polite - Showing good manners and respect toward others.

> The team greeted the clients warmly using polite language.

Formal - Following established conventions or rules, often in a professional context.

The language used during the meeting was formal.

Presentation - A talk or display designed to inform or persuade an audience.

The team prepared a clear and easy-to-follow presentation.

Visuals - Images, charts, or diagrams used to illustrate information.

The presentation included visuals to support their points.

Thoughtful - Showing careful consideration or attention.

The clients asked thoughtful questions during the meeting.

Active - Engaged and attentive in the process of communication or participation.

Rachel made sure to listen actively to the clients.

Non-verbal - Communication without using spoken words, such as body language or facial expressions.

The team paid attention to non-verbal cues during the presentation.

Professionalism - The competence, skill, and behavior expected of a professional.

The clients were impressed with the team's professionalism.

Collaboration - The action of working together to achieve a common goal.

The meeting ended with agreements on future collaboration.

Success - The achievement of a desired outcome or result.

The meeting was both a business success and a learning experience.

24.

THE OFFICE MOVE

When the announcement came that the office was moving to a new location, everyone was both excited and anxious. The old office had been comfortable, but the company needed more space and better facilities. Rachel, the office manager, began planning the move immediately.

"Moving is always a challenge," Rachel said at the team meeting. "We'll need to adapt to new surroundings and adjust our workflows to fit the new office layout. But I'm confident that we can manage it smoothly."

The first step was packing up the old office. The team gathered boxes and packing materials, and everyone began sorting through their desks. Some items were clearly marked for disposal, while others were carefully packed to be taken to the new location. The packing process was time-consuming but necessary.

James, one of the team members, took charge of labeling the boxes. "We need to make sure everything is properly labeled so that we can find it easily in the new office," he explained. "It will help us stay organized and avoid any confusion."

After a few days of packing, the moving day arrived. The office movers came early in the morning, and the team watched as their belongings were loaded onto the truck. It was a big job, but the movers were efficient and professional.

When the team arrived at the new office, they were greeted with a fresh, modern space. The new office had an open layout with plenty of natural light, which was a big change from the old, dimly lit rooms. The team began unpacking and setting up their workstations. Rachel had arranged for some temporary workspaces to be set up quickly so that the team could continue working while the final touches were completed.

The first few days in the new office were busy. The team had to adjust to the new environment and find their way around. Some of the equipment was different, and there were new procedures to learn. Despite the initial confusion, everyone worked together to get settled in.

As the weeks went by, the team adapted to their new surroundings. They found ways to make the most of the open layout, and productivity gradually improved. The new office also offered some great amenities, like a larger break room and more meeting spaces, which everyone appreciated.

Rachel called a team meeting to gather feedback. "How is everyone adjusting to the new office?" she asked. "Do you have any suggestions for making things even better?"

The team shared their thoughts and ideas, and Rachel took note of their suggestions. Overall, the feedback was positive. The team was pleased with the new office and felt that the move had been a success.

By the end of the month, the team was fully settled in. The new office had become a comfortable and efficient workspace. Rachel felt proud of how well the team had handled the transition, and she was excited about the opportunities that the new location offered.

Announcement - An important public statement or declaration.

- The announcement about the office move came as a surprise to the team.

Location - A particular place or position.

- The office was moving to a new location with better

facilities.

Surroundings - The environment or conditions around a person or thing.

- The team had to adapt to new surroundings in the new office.

Workflow - The sequence of processes through which a piece of work passes from initiation to completion.

- The team needed to adjust their workflows to fit the new office layout.

Packing - The act of putting things into boxes or containers for moving.

- The team spent days packing up the old office.

Materials - Items needed for a specific purpose, such as packing.

- They gathered boxes and packing materials for the move.

Labeling - The act of putting labels on items for identification.

- James took charge of labeling the boxes to keep everything organized.

Efficient - Performing tasks in the best possible manner with the least waste of time and effort.

- The movers were efficient and completed the job quickly.

Modern - Relating to the present or recent times; up-to-date.

- The new office had a fresh, modern design with plenty of natural light.

Workspace - An area or environment where work is done.

- The team began setting up their workstations in the new office.

Productivity - The effectiveness of productive effort, measured in terms of the rate of output per unit of input.

- Productivity gradually improved as the team adapted to the new office.

Amenities - Features or facilities that make a place more comfortable or enjoyable.

- The new office offered great amenities like a larger break room.

Transition - The process of changing from one state or condition to another.

- Rachel felt proud of how well the team handled the transition.

Settled - Being comfortable and established in a new situation or place.

- By the end of the month, the team was fully settled in the new office.

Feedback - Information or opinions about how well something is working.

- Rachel called a meeting to gather feedback on the new office.

Suggestion - An idea or proposal offered for consideration.

- The team shared their suggestions for making the new office even better.

Comfortable - Providing physical ease and relaxation.

- The new office became a comfortable and efficient workspace.

Efficient - Able to accomplish a task without wasted effort or expense.

- The new office layout helped the team be more efficient in their work.

Professional - Showing high standards of work and behavior.

- The movers were professional and ensured everything was handled carefully.

Organized - Arranged or structured in a systematic way.

- Proper labeling kept the packing process organized and efficient.

25.

THE CONFLICT RESOLUTION

Claire was a team leader known for her calm demeanor and fairness. One morning, she arrived at the office to find two colleagues, Alex and Sam, in a heated discussion by the coffee machine. Their disagreement was disrupting the office atmosphere, and Claire knew she needed to step in.

"What's going on here?" Claire asked, trying to sound neutral.

Alex and Sam stopped talking and glanced at her. Alex was clearly frustrated. "Sam and I have been having issues with our project deadlines. Sam thinks I'm not pulling my weight, but I believe I'm doing my part."

Sam nodded in agreement. "Alex is often late with his reports, and it's affecting my ability to complete my tasks on time. It's been an ongoing issue."

Claire listened carefully. She understood that resolving conflicts required more than just hearing both sides; it required finding a solution that worked for everyone involved.

"Okay, let's sit down and discuss this calmly," Claire suggested. She led them to a nearby meeting room where they could talk without interruptions.

Once they were seated, Claire began by setting some ground rules. "First, we need to speak respectfully and listen to each other's points of view. Let's focus on finding a solution rather than placing blame."

Alex and Sam agreed, and Claire encouraged them to express their concerns openly. Alex explained that he had been struggling with personal issues that affected his work schedule. Sam, on the other hand, revealed that the delays were impacting his own deadlines, creating a lot of stress.

Claire nodded understandingly. "It sounds like both of you have valid concerns. How about we work together to come up with a plan that addresses these issues?"

Alex and Sam agreed to create a more detailed project schedule. They decided to have regular check-ins to ensure that both were on track. Alex also promised to communicate better about any delays, and Sam agreed to be more flexible with the deadlines when possible.

The meeting concluded with both colleagues feeling more positive about the situation. Claire emphasized the importance of teamwork and communication in resolving conflicts.

A few weeks later, the project was back on track, and Alex and Sam's working relationship had improved significantly. Claire was pleased with the outcome and felt satisfied that she had helped resolve the conflict in a constructive manner.

Demeanor - The way a person behaves towards others.
- Claire was known for her calm demeanor, which helped her handle difficult situations.

Disagreement - A situation where people have different opinions or views.
- A disagreement arose between Alex and Sam over their project deadlines.

Heated - Showing strong feelings, often anger.
- Alex and Sam were having a heated discussion about their work.

Neutral - Not supporting any side in a conflict.

- Claire tried to sound neutral when she asked about the problem.

Disrupting - Causing disturbance or interruption.

- The disagreement was disrupting the office atmosphere.

Colleagues - People who work together in the same organization.

- Alex and Sam were colleagues who had a disagreement over their work.

Fairness - Treating people equally and justly.

- Claire was known for her fairness in handling team issues.

Issue - A problem or concern that needs to be addressed.

- The team was facing issues with meeting their project deadlines.

Ground Rules - Basic rules or principles for conduct in a situation.

- Claire set some ground rules for the meeting to ensure respectful communication.

Respectfully - In a way that shows respect for others.

- Claire asked Alex and Sam to speak respectfully during their discussion.

Points of View - Perspectives or opinions on a matter.

- Claire encouraged them to listen to each other's points of view.

Solution - An answer to a problem or difficulty.

- They worked together to find a solution to their conflict.

Valid - Legally or logically acceptable; reasonable.

- Claire acknowledged that both Alex and Sam had valid concerns.

Schedule - A plan of when tasks or events will occur.

- They decided to create a more detailed project schedule.

Check-ins - Meetings or updates to review progress.

- Alex and Sam agreed to have regular check-ins to monitor their progress.

Flexible - Able to change or adapt easily.

- Sam agreed to be more flexible with deadlines when possible.

Teamwork - Collaborative effort of a group to achieve a goal.

- Claire emphasized the importance of teamwork in resolving conflicts.

Constructive - Helping to improve or develop.

- The conflict resolution was approached in a constructive manner.

Relationship - The way in which two or more people or groups feel and behave towards each other.

- Alex and Sam's working relationship improved after resolving their conflict.

Outcome - The result or effect of an action or situation.

- Claire was pleased with the outcome of the conflict resolution.

26.

THE BUDGET MEETING

Sarah had been working at the company for just over a year and was excited to attend her first budget meeting. She knew this meeting was crucial because it would determine how the company's finances would be allocated for the next quarter. The room was filled with managers and financial analysts who all seemed to be focused on their laptops and piles of documents.

As the meeting began, Mr. Thompson, the head of the finance department, started by outlining the agenda. "Today, we'll review our current financial status, discuss the budget proposals, and make decisions about where to allocate funds."

Sarah listened intently as Mr. Thompson explained the key business metrics. "We need to look at our revenue, expenses, and profit margins to understand our financial health. Revenue is how much money we make, expenses are the costs we incur, and profit margin is the percentage of revenue that turns into profit."

One by one, the managers presented their budget proposals. Each proposal included detailed projections about future expenses and expected returns on investments. Sarah was impressed by how meticulously they had prepared their reports. It was clear that understanding these metrics was essential for making informed decisions.

When it was Sarah's turn to present her budget proposal for the marketing department, she felt a mix of excitement and nervousness. She had prepared a detailed plan, outlining how the proposed budget would be used to enhance the company's brand visibility and attract new clients. Her proposal included specific figures for advertising costs, promotional events, and market research.

Mr. Thompson asked several questions about her projections. "Can you explain why you believe these figures are realistic?" he asked. Sarah confidently explained the market research she had conducted and how it supported her budget plan.

After everyone had presented, the team discussed the proposals and debated where to allocate resources most effectively. They had to consider various factors, such as the potential return on investment and the impact on different departments.

The meeting ended with a consensus on the budget allocations. Sarah felt relieved and proud of how well her presentation had gone. She realized that financial planning was not just about numbers; it was about understanding how to use those numbers to make strategic decisions for the company's future.

As the team wrapped up, Mr. Thompson thanked everyone for their hard work and contributions. "Effective financial planning and understanding these key metrics are essential for our success. Let's put these plans into action and monitor our progress."

Sarah left the meeting feeling more knowledgeable and confident about her role in the company. She understood that budget meetings were a crucial part of ensuring the company's financial stability and growth.

Crucial - Extremely important or necessary.

> The budget meeting was crucial for deciding the company's financial direction.

Allocate - To distribute or assign resources or tasks to different areas.

The team discussed how to allocate funds for various departments.

Outline - To give a general description or plan of something.

Mr. Thompson outlined the agenda for the budget meeting.

Metrics - Measurements or standards used to evaluate performance.

Key business metrics include revenue, expenses, and profit margins.

Revenue - The total amount of money received by a business from its activities.

Revenue is how much money the company makes before expenses are deducted.

Expenses - The costs incurred in the process of earning revenue.

Expenses include things like salaries, rent, and utility bills.

Profit Margin - The percentage of revenue that remains after all expenses are subtracted.

The profit margin indicates how much profit the company makes from each dollar of revenue.

Proposal - A plan or suggestion put forward for consideration or discussion.

Each manager presented a budget proposal detailing their financial needs.

Projections - Estimates or forecasts of future financial performance.

The budget proposal included projections for future expenses and returns.

Meticulously - With great attention to detail and accuracy.

The managers had prepared their reports meticulously to

ensure accuracy.

Informed - Based on knowledge or information.

Making informed decisions requires understanding financial metrics.

Enhance - To improve or increase the quality or value of something.

Sarah's proposal aimed to enhance the company's brand visibility.

Promotional - Related to activities that advertise or market a product or service.

The budget included costs for promotional events to attract new clients.

Market Research - The process of gathering and analyzing information about consumer needs and preferences.

Sarah conducted market research to support her budget proposal.

Consensus - General agreement among a group of people.

The meeting ended with a consensus on how to allocate the budget.

Strategic - Related to long-term planning and decision-making.

Financial planning is crucial for making strategic decisions about the company's future.

Stability - The state of being steady and unchanging.

Effective financial planning helps ensure the company's financial stability.

Growth - The process of increasing in size, amount, or importance.

The budget aimed to support the company's growth by

investing in key areas.

Contributions - The input or efforts provided by individuals to achieve a common goal.

Mr. Thompson thanked everyone for their contributions to the budget discussion.

Knowledgeable - Possessing a lot of information or understanding about a subject.

Sarah felt more knowledgeable about financial planning after the meeting.

27.

THE BRAINSTORMING SESSION

The marketing team at Bright Ideas Inc. was gearing up for a major project. Their task was to come up with a new campaign to promote their latest product. To do this, they scheduled a brainstorming session, which was known to be both exciting and challenging.

On the day of the session, the room was filled with anticipation. Lisa, the team leader, started the meeting by encouraging everyone to share their ideas without hesitation. "Remember, there are no bad ideas in brainstorming. We want to hear everything you've got!"

David, a junior marketer, was the first to speak up. "What if we use a series of short videos that showcase real customers using the product? We could make it funny and relatable."

"That's a great idea!" Lisa said, jotting it down on the whiteboard. "What else?"

Sophia, who had a background in graphic design, suggested, "How about using interactive social media posts? We could create polls and quizzes to engage our audience and get them involved."

Tom, the team's content writer, added, "We could also host a live Q&A session with the product's developers. This way, customers can ask questions directly and learn more about the product."

As the ideas flowed, Lisa made sure to listen carefully and

take notes. She knew that the best campaigns often came from combining various perspectives. The team discussed each idea, building on them and considering how they could work together.

In the middle of the session, Maria, who was quiet for most of the meeting, finally spoke up. "What if we create a series of behind-the-scenes videos that show the making of the product? People love to see how things are made."

Lisa was excited by this suggestion. "I love that idea, Maria. It adds a personal touch and can make our campaign stand out."

The team continued brainstorming, mixing and matching ideas until they had a solid plan. They decided to create a combination of video content, interactive posts, and behind-the-scenes footage. Each team member contributed their unique skills, and together they developed a creative and engaging campaign.

At the end of the session, Lisa thanked everyone for their contributions. "You've all done a fantastic job. By working together and considering different viewpoints, we've come up with a campaign that will really make an impact."

As the team left the room, they felt a sense of accomplishment. They had learned that brainstorming was not just about generating ideas but also about collaborating and valuing each other's input. They were excited to put their plan into action and see the results.

Brainstorming - The process of thinking of as many ideas as possible to solve a problem.

- The team used brainstorming to come up with creative ideas for their marketing campaign.

Campaign - A series of actions intended to achieve a particular result, especially in advertising or marketing.

- They developed a new campaign to promote their latest

product.

Encouraging - Giving someone confidence or support.

- Lisa was encouraging everyone to share their ideas without hesitation.

Hesitation - A pause before doing something, often due to uncertainty.

- Lisa wanted the team to speak up without hesitation.

Relatable - Easy to understand and connect with because it is familiar or similar to one's own experience.

- David's idea was to make the videos funny and relatable.

Interactive - Involving active participation and engagement from users.

- Sophia suggested using interactive social media posts to engage the audience.

Engage - To involve or attract interest.

- Interactive posts are designed to engage the audience and get them involved.

Q&A - A session where questions are answered, often following a presentation or speech.

- Tom proposed hosting a live Q&A session with the product's developers.

Developers - People who design or create something, such as software or products.

- Customers could ask questions directly to the product's developers.

Behind-the-scenes - Referring to activities that are not visible to the public but are essential to the process.

- Maria suggested creating behind-the-scenes videos of the product's making.

Perspective - A particular way of thinking about something or a point of view.

- The team valued each other's perspectives during the brainstorming session.

Contribute - To give or add something in order to help achieve a goal.

- Each team member contributed their unique skills to the campaign.

Unique - One of a kind or unlike anything else.

- The campaign was designed to showcase their unique approach.

Solid - Strong or reliable; not easily broken or undermined.

- They had a solid plan by combining various ideas.

Accomplishment - Something achieved successfully, often through effort.

- The team felt a sense of accomplishment after the brainstorming session.

Collaboration - Working together with others to achieve a common goal.

- The campaign was successful due to the team's effective collaboration.

Input - Contributions or ideas provided by people in a group.

- The team valued everyone's input during the brainstorming session.

Jot - To write something quickly and briefly.

- Lisa jotted down each idea on the whiteboard.

Build on - To use an idea or suggestion as a starting point for further development.

- They built on each idea, combining them to create a

complete campaign.

Mixing and matching - Combining different elements or ideas to create something new.

- The team mixed and matched ideas to develop their campaign.

28.

THE SALES PITCH

Alex was preparing for an important sales pitch. He had been working at his company for a few years, but this was his first chance to present to a large potential client. He knew this opportunity could make a big difference in his career, so he wanted to get it right.

The night before the pitch, Alex reviewed his notes and practiced his presentation multiple times. He had researched the client's company thoroughly and understood their needs and preferences. He wanted to make sure his pitch would address these needs clearly and effectively.

On the day of the pitch, Alex arrived at the client's office early. He was nervous but determined. As he set up his laptop and projector, he reminded himself of the key points he wanted to cover. His goal was to persuade the client that his company's product was the best solution for their needs.

When the meeting started, Alex greeted the client warmly. "Good morning! Thank you for having me here today. I'm excited to present how our product can benefit your company."

The client, Mr. Thompson, smiled and nodded. "We're looking forward to hearing your pitch, Alex."

Alex began his presentation with a strong opening. He highlighted the main benefits of the product and used clear visuals to support his points. "Our product is designed to improve efficiency and reduce costs. It has been successful in several similar companies, and we believe it can offer the same results for you."

As he continued, Alex addressed potential concerns and questions before they were even raised. "I know that one of your main concerns might be the initial investment. However, the long-term savings and increased productivity will quickly outweigh the initial costs."

Mr. Thompson listened attentively. Alex could see that his words were having an impact. To build more trust, Alex shared testimonials from other satisfied clients. "Here are some examples of how our product has helped businesses like yours."

Throughout the pitch, Alex made sure to engage with Mr. Thompson. He asked questions to gauge his interest and encouraged him to share his thoughts. "Do you have any specific requirements or concerns that we haven't covered yet?"

By the end of the presentation, Alex felt confident that he had made a strong case. Mr. Thompson seemed impressed and asked a few detailed questions about the implementation process. Alex answered them clearly and assured him that his company would provide full support during the transition.

After the meeting, Alex thanked Mr. Thompson for his time. "I appreciate the opportunity to present to you today. If you have any further questions or need additional information, please don't hesitate to contact me."

As Alex left the office, he felt a sense of accomplishment. He had used his preparation and presentation skills to deliver a persuasive pitch. He hoped that his efforts would lead to a successful deal and an exciting new chapter in his career.

Pitch - A presentation or proposal intended to persuade others.
- Alex prepared carefully for his sales pitch to win over the potential client.

Persuade - To convince someone to believe or do something.

- Alex used various techniques to persuade the client that his product was the best choice.

Opportunity - A chance for advancement or improvement.

- This was Alex's first opportunity to present to a large potential client.

Client - A person or company that receives services from a professional.

- Alex was preparing to meet with a potential client named Mr. Thompson.

Thoroughly - In a detailed and careful way.

- Alex researched the client's company thoroughly before the pitch.

Address - To deal with or discuss a particular issue.

- Alex addressed the client's potential concerns before they were even raised.

Concerns - Worries or issues that need to be considered.

- Alex anticipated the client's concerns about the initial investment.

Testimonial - A statement from a satisfied customer or user.

- Alex shared testimonials from other clients to build trust.

Implementation - The process of putting a plan or product into action.

- Mr. Thompson asked about the implementation process of the product.

Engage - To involve someone in a conversation or activity.

- Alex engaged with Mr. Thompson by asking questions and encouraging feedback.

Transition - The process of changing from one state to another.

- Alex assured Mr. Thompson that his company would support the transition.

Accomplishment - A successful achievement or completion of a task.

- Alex felt a sense of accomplishment after delivering his pitch.

Confident - Feeling sure of oneself and one's abilities.

- Alex felt confident that he had made a strong case during the pitch.

Greet - To welcome someone with a polite expression or gesture.

- Alex greeted Mr. Thompson warmly at the start of the meeting.

Visuals - Images or diagrams used to illustrate or support information.

- Alex used clear visuals to support his points during the presentation.

Support - To assist or provide help.

- Alex promised that his company would provide full support during the implementation.

Requirements - Necessary conditions or specifications.

- Alex asked if there were any specific requirements or concerns that needed to be addressed.

Detailed - Including a lot of information and specifics.

- Alex answered Mr. Thompson's detailed questions about the product.

Impressed - Feeling admiration or respect due to something well done.

- Mr. Thompson seemed impressed with Alex's presentation.

Accomplished - Successful in achieving a goal or task.
- Alex felt accomplished after the successful pitch.

29.

THE ANNUAL REVIEW

Emily was preparing for her annual review at work. This was a significant moment because it would determine how she had performed over the past year and set the direction for her future growth. She knew that feedback from her manager, Mr. Johnson, would help her understand her strengths and areas for improvement.

The day of the review arrived, and Emily felt a mix of excitement and nervousness. She had worked hard over the past year and hoped that her efforts would be recognized. As she walked into Mr. Johnson's office, she greeted him with a smile. "Good morning, Mr. Johnson. I'm ready for our review."

Mr. Johnson smiled back. "Good morning, Emily. Let's get started. I've been looking forward to discussing your progress."

Emily sat down and listened attentively as Mr. Johnson began to talk about her performance. He started by highlighting her achievements. "You've done a great job on several projects this year. Your attention to detail and commitment have really stood out."

Emily felt a sense of pride as she heard this. She had put a lot of effort into her work, and it was gratifying to know that it was appreciated.

However, Mr. Johnson also mentioned some areas where Emily could improve. "There are a few areas where I think you can grow. For instance, improving your communication skills could help you work more effectively with the team."

Emily listened carefully, taking notes. She understood that receiving constructive criticism was part of the review process and saw it as an opportunity to learn and develop. "Thank you for the feedback. I'll work on improving my communication skills."

Mr. Johnson then asked Emily about her goals for the coming year. "What goals would you like to set for yourself? It's important to have clear objectives to focus on."

Emily thought about this for a moment. "I'd like to set a goal to lead more projects and take on additional responsibilities. I also want to improve my skills in project management."

Mr. Johnson nodded in approval. "Those are excellent goals. Setting clear and achievable objectives will help you grow professionally. Let's make a plan to support you in reaching these goals."

They discussed a plan for Emily's professional development, including training opportunities and regular check-ins to monitor her progress. Emily felt encouraged by the support and resources that would be available to her.

As the review concluded, Mr. Johnson offered some final words of encouragement. "Overall, you've had a strong year. Keep up the good work and continue striving for improvement."

Emily thanked Mr. Johnson and left the meeting feeling motivated. She was ready to tackle her new goals and use the feedback to enhance her skills. She knew that with dedication and hard work, she could achieve her professional aspirations.

Review - An assessment or evaluation of performance.

- Emily was preparing for her annual review to discuss her performance.

Significant - Important or notable.

- The annual review was a significant moment for Emily's career.

Feedback - Information about how one is performing, used to improve.

- Emily listened carefully to the feedback from Mr. Johnson.

Achievement - A successful accomplishment of a task or goal.

- Mr. Johnson highlighted Emily's achievements in her review.

Strengths - Positive qualities or abilities.

- Emily was pleased to hear about her strengths during the review.

Improvement - The process of getting better at something.

- Mr. Johnson suggested areas for improvement, such as communication skills.

Constructive - Helpful and intended to improve.

- Emily appreciated the constructive criticism she received.

Objective - A goal or target that one aims to achieve.

- Emily set clear objectives for herself for the coming year.

Responsibility - Duties or tasks that one is required to manage.

- Emily wanted to take on additional responsibilities to grow professionally.

Encouraged - Given support or confidence to do something.

- Emily felt encouraged by the support and resources provided.

Development - The process of improving skills or knowledge.

- They discussed a plan for Emily's professional development.

Training - Instruction or practice to improve skills.

- Emily would have the opportunity for training to enhance her abilities.

Motivated - Driven to take action or achieve goals.

- Emily left the meeting feeling motivated to achieve her new goals.

Dedication - Commitment to a task or purpose.

- With dedication and hard work, Emily hoped to achieve her professional aspirations.

Aspirations - Ambitions or goals that one aims to reach.

- Emily was determined to reach her professional aspirations.

30.

THE BUSINESS TRIP

The team was excited about their upcoming business trip to Berlin. It was a chance to meet with international clients and learn more about conducting business in different cultures. Emma, the team leader, emphasized the importance of understanding travel etiquette and being well-prepared.

As the team gathered at the airport, Emma reminded everyone of a few key points. "Remember, when traveling abroad, it's crucial to be polite and respectful of local customs. Make sure to familiarize yourself with basic cultural norms before we arrive."

The flight was long, but everyone was eager to start their trip. Once they landed in Berlin, they quickly noticed the city's unique charm. The team checked into their hotel and had a brief meeting to discuss the next day's agenda. Emma stressed the need for punctuality. "We have a busy schedule, so let's make sure we are always on time for our meetings."

The next day, the team met with their German counterparts. Emma introduced everyone and made sure to use formal greetings. The clients appreciated the effort and responded positively. Emma had advised her team to dress professionally, and it paid off. The clients were impressed with their polished appearance and respectful behavior.

During the meetings, the team discussed various projects and exchanged ideas. Emma made sure that everyone had a chance to speak and encouraged active participation. She also reminded her colleagues to listen carefully and avoid interrupting. "Effective communication is key. Make sure to express your ideas clearly and be open to others' opinions."

In the evenings, the team explored Berlin's famous landmarks. They visited the Brandenburg Gate, walked along the Berlin Wall, and enjoyed local cuisine. Emma reminded everyone to use polite phrases when interacting with locals, such as "please" and "thank you." This small gesture helped the team build rapport with the people they met.

On the final day of their trip, the team had a debriefing session to reflect on their experience. Emma praised everyone for their professionalism and adaptability. "We managed to conduct successful meetings and made a good impression. Your preparation and respectful behavior were key to our success."

The trip was a valuable learning experience for the team. They returned home with a greater understanding of international business etiquette and the importance of being well-prepared. Emma encouraged them to apply these lessons in future projects and maintain the positive relationships they had built.

Etiquette - The customary code of polite behavior in society or among professionals.

> It's crucial to understand travel etiquette when visiting a new country.

Customs - Traditional practices or behaviors typical of a particular country or people.

> Familiarize yourself with basic customs before arriving in a new place.

Punctuality - Being on time.

> Emma stressed the need for punctuality to ensure a smooth schedule.

Counterparts - People or organizations that have similar roles or positions in different places.

The team met with their German counterparts to discuss the project.

Formal - Adhering to established conventions or customs, especially in behavior or dress.

Emma advised her team to dress formally for the business meetings.

Polished - Showing a high level of sophistication and refinement.

The clients were impressed with the team's polished appearance and behavior.

Participate - To take part in or become involved in an activity.

Emma encouraged active participation during the meetings.

Rapport - A positive and harmonious relationship.

Using polite phrases helped the team build rapport with locals.

Debriefing - A meeting to review and discuss what happened after an event.

The team had a debriefing session to reflect on their trip.

Professionalism - The competence or skill expected of a professional.

Emma praised the team's professionalism and adaptability during the trip.

Adaptability - The ability to adjust to new conditions.

The team showed great adaptability in handling various situations abroad.

Respectful - Showing politeness and regard for others.

The team's respectful behavior was appreciated by their clients.

Gesture - A movement or action that conveys a particular meaning.

Saying "please" and "thank you" is a simple but effective gesture.

Impression - The effect or impact made on someone.

The team made a positive impression with their professional demeanor.

Success - The accomplishment of an aim or purpose.

The trip was considered a success due to the team's effective communication and preparation.

31.

THE NEW POLICY

The team gathered in the conference room, where the new company policy was about to be announced. Emma, the HR manager, stood at the front with a serious expression. She began, "As you know, the company is implementing a new policy that will affect all departments. I understand there may be some confusion, so I'm here to clarify everything."

The new policy was designed to improve efficiency, but it also meant significant changes in how things were done. Emma explained, "Firstly, we are introducing flexible working hours. This means you can start your day anytime between 7 a.m. and 10 a.m. and finish accordingly."

This announcement caused a buzz among the team. Many were excited about the flexibility but concerned about how it would impact their schedules and team meetings. Emma continued, "Secondly, we will be transitioning to a new project management system. This system is supposed to streamline our processes and enhance communication."

Alex, one of the team members, raised his hand. "How will this new system change our daily tasks?"

Emma replied, "The new system will require you to update your tasks and track progress online. This will help us stay organized and make it easier to see how projects are progressing."

Jessica, another team member, looked worried. "What about the team meetings? Will they still be held at the same times?"

Emma assured her, "Yes, the team meetings will remain at the same times. However, we will be using the new system to share meeting agendas and documents."

As the meeting continued, Emma addressed various concerns and questions from the team. She provided examples of how the new policy would work in practice and gave tips on how to adapt to the changes. "I know this is a lot to take in," she said, "but remember that these changes are meant to help us work more efficiently and improve our overall productivity."

The team was given a week to familiarize themselves with the new policy and the project management system. Emma organized training sessions to help everyone get up to speed. The sessions were interactive and allowed team members to ask questions and practice using the new tools.

By the end of the week, the team had adjusted to the new policy. Although there were initial challenges, they found the new system to be beneficial. Flexibility in working hours allowed everyone to manage their time better, and the new project management system made collaboration easier.

Emma concluded, "I appreciate your patience and adaptability during this transition. The new policy will help us improve our work environment and achieve better results."

Confusion - A lack of clarity or understanding.
- The new policy caused confusion among the team members.

Implications - The possible effects or consequences of something.
- Understanding the implications of the new policy was important for the team.

Flexible - Able to change or adapt easily.
- The new policy introduced flexible working hours for the

employees.

Transitioning - The process of changing from one state or condition to another.

- We will be transitioning to a new project management system.

Streamline - To make something more efficient by simplifying it.

- The new system is supposed to streamline our processes.

Enhance - To improve or make something better.

- The new system will enhance communication within the team.

Track - To monitor or follow the progress of something.

- The new system allows us to track the progress of our projects.

Organized - Arranged or structured in a systematic way.

- The new system will help us stay organized.

Productivity - The effectiveness of effort or work.

- The changes are meant to improve our overall productivity.

Familiarize - To become acquainted with something through experience.

- The team was given a week to familiarize themselves with the new policy.

Adapt - To adjust to new conditions or changes.

- The team had to adapt to the new working hours and system.

Interactive - Involving active participation or engagement.

- The training sessions were interactive, allowing team members to practice the new tools.

Collaboration - Working together towards a common goal.

- The new system made collaboration easier among team members.

Patience - The ability to remain calm and wait without frustration.

- Emma appreciated the team's patience during the transition.

Transition - The process of changing from one state or condition to another.

- The transition to the new policy was smooth after the training sessions.

32.

THE PRODUCT FEEDBACK

The team at InnovateTech was excited about their new product launch. They had worked hard for months on the latest gadget, a smart home assistant designed to make daily tasks easier. Now, it was time to gather feedback from their first customers.

Sarah, the product manager, organized a feedback session. She welcomed the participants with a warm smile and explained, "We really appreciate you taking the time to test our new product. Your feedback is crucial for us to understand what works and what doesn't."

The participants were given the smart home assistants and asked to use them for a week. They were encouraged to note down their thoughts and experiences. Some of the key areas Sarah wanted feedback on included ease of use, functionality, and design.

After a week, the team gathered the participants again for a review meeting. Each person shared their experiences, both positive and negative. John, one of the testers, mentioned, "I love the voice recognition feature. It's very accurate and responsive. However, I found the setup process a bit confusing."

Another participant, Emma, added, "The design is sleek and modern, but the assistant has trouble connecting to my other smart devices. It would be great if it could sync better."

The team listened carefully to each comment. Sarah took

detailed notes, making sure to capture both the strengths and weaknesses of the product. "Thank you for your honest feedback," she said. "We'll use these insights to make improvements."

The next step was to analyze the feedback and identify common issues. The team held a brainstorming session to discuss potential solutions. They decided to focus on improving the setup process and enhancing the device's compatibility with other smart products.

After implementing the changes, the team planned another round of testing to ensure the issues were resolved. Sarah explained to the team, "It's important to continue listening to our customers and refining our product until we get it right."

In the end, the improved smart home assistant received positive reviews. The team was pleased with the progress and grateful for the valuable feedback they received. They understood that customer input was essential for creating a successful product.

The experience taught them that gathering and acting on feedback was a vital part of product development. They were excited to continue making products that truly met their customers' needs.

Feedback - Information or opinions about how something can be improved.

- Sarah appreciated the participants' feedback on the new product.

Functionality - The quality of being able to perform a task or function.

- The team wanted feedback on the product's functionality.

Design - The way something is planned and made to look.

- Emma liked the sleek design of the smart home assistant.

Participants - People who take part in an activity or event.

- The participants tested the new product and provided their opinions.

Experience - The knowledge or skill acquired through practical involvement.

- John shared his experience with the smart home assistant.

Accurate - Correct and precise.

- The voice recognition feature was very accurate and responsive.

Confusing - Difficult to understand or follow.

- John found the setup process a bit confusing.

Sleek - Smooth and elegant in appearance.

- The design of the smart home assistant was sleek and modern.

Connecting - Linking or joining together.

- Emma mentioned the device had trouble connecting to her other smart devices.

Sync - To work together harmoniously or match.

- The team aimed to improve the device's ability to sync with other products.

Analyze - To examine something in detail to understand it better.

- The team analyzed the feedback to identify common issues.

Brainstorming - Generating ideas or solutions through group discussion.

- The team held a brainstorming session to find solutions for the issues.

Refine - To improve something by making small changes.

- They continued refining the product based on the feedback they received.

Essential - Absolutely necessary or very important.

- Gathering and acting on feedback was essential for product development.

Valuable - Useful or important.

- The feedback they received was valuable for improving the product.

33.

THE SUSTAINABILITY INITIATIVE

When GreenTech Corporation decided to launch their new sustainability initiative, everyone in the office was excited but also a bit uncertain. The goal was to make the company more environmentally friendly and reduce its carbon footprint.

Laura, the head of the initiative, gathered the team for an important meeting. "Our new sustainability program aims to minimize our impact on the environment," she explained. "We need to learn and implement some eco-friendly practices."

The meeting began with Laura introducing the key areas of focus: recycling, energy efficiency, and reducing waste. Each department was assigned a specific task to help the company reach its goals. For instance, the IT department would focus on reducing electronic waste, while the facilities team would work on conserving energy.

Tom, from the marketing team, was curious about how he could contribute. Laura encouraged him to think about ways to promote sustainability in their campaigns. "You can help by creating awareness about our new practices," she said. "We need to make sure our clients and partners understand our commitment to the environment."

The next few weeks were busy as everyone started working on their tasks. The recycling bins were placed around the office, and clear labels were put on them to help employees sort their waste properly. The company also started using energy-efficient light bulbs and encouraged everyone to turn off lights and equipment when not in use.

Emily, from the HR department, organized a workshop to educate employees about sustainable practices. She invited a guest speaker who specialized in environmental science. The workshop was informative, covering topics like the importance of reducing plastic use and the benefits of using reusable items.

One day, Laura noticed that the office was looking cleaner and more organized. She saw that people were getting better at separating recyclables from general waste. She was pleased with the progress but knew there was still more work to be done.

Laura decided to hold a feedback session to gather opinions from the team. She asked everyone what they thought of the new practices and if they had any suggestions for improvement. The feedback was mostly positive, with many employees expressing appreciation for the new initiatives.

Tom shared his thoughts: "I think our recycling efforts are going well. However, we might need more bins for different types of recyclables, like paper and plastic."

Emily suggested: "It would be helpful to have more frequent reminders about turning off unused equipment. Maybe we could set up a monthly email with tips on sustainability."

Laura took all the feedback into account and made a plan to address the suggestions. She updated the recycling stations and arranged for regular sustainability tips to be sent out.

The company continued to make strides in its sustainability goals. Laura was thrilled to see that not only were the employees participating actively, but they were also becoming more conscious of their environmental impact.

In the end, the initiative was a success, and GreenTech Corporation became known for its commitment to sustainability. The team learned that small changes in daily habits could make a big difference. Laura felt proud of the progress and was excited to see how the company would continue to grow in its efforts to protect the environment.

Sustainability - The ability to maintain or support an activity over the long term, often focusing on environmental preservation.
- The company's sustainability initiative aimed to reduce its carbon footprint.

Initiative - A new plan or strategy intended to achieve a particular goal.
- Laura explained the new sustainability initiative to the team.

Eco-friendly - Having a minimal impact on the environment.
- The company implemented eco-friendly practices to reduce waste.

Footprint - The impact or effect that something has on the environment.
- The goal was to minimize the company's carbon footprint.

Recycling - The process of converting waste into reusable material.
- Recycling bins were placed around the office to encourage sorting waste.

Efficiency - The ability to do something effectively without wasting resources.
- The team focused on energy efficiency by using LED light bulbs.

Waste - Unwanted or unusable material that is discarded.
- The company aimed to reduce waste by improving their recycling practices.

Conserving - The act of protecting or saving resources, such as energy or water.

- The facilities team worked on conserving energy throughout the office.

Campaigns - Organized efforts to promote a particular cause or product.

- Tom was tasked with promoting sustainability in the company's campaigns.

Awareness - Knowledge or understanding of a particular issue or situation.

- The workshop helped raise awareness about sustainable practices.

Educate - To teach or inform someone about a particular subject.

- Emily organized a workshop to educate employees on environmental science.

Feedback - Opinions or suggestions about how something can be improved.

- Laura held a feedback session to gather opinions from the team.

Conscious - Being aware of and concerned about a particular issue.

- Employees became more conscious of their environmental impact.

Contribute - To give or add something in order to help achieve a goal.

- Tom wanted to contribute to the sustainability efforts by creating awareness.

Implement - To put a plan or decision into effect.

- The company implemented new recycling bins and energy-saving measures.

34.

THE TRAINING SESSION

At TechWorld Inc., the introduction of a new software system was creating a buzz among employees. The company had scheduled a training session to ensure everyone was up to speed with the new program.

Alex, the training coordinator, stood at the front of the conference room. The room was filled with employees, all eager but also a little anxious about learning the new system. Alex started the session with a warm welcome. "Thank you all for coming today. This new software will help us work more efficiently, but it requires a bit of training to get used to it."

The first part of the session involved a detailed demonstration of the software's features. Alex clicked through various screens, explaining how each function worked. "This dashboard," Alex pointed to the screen, "is where you'll find all the key tools you need for your daily tasks. It might seem complex at first, but with practice, it will become second nature."

Emma, from the sales team, raised her hand. "How will this new system affect our workflow?" she asked. Alex smiled and answered, "Great question, Emma. The system is designed to streamline our processes, which means less time spent on repetitive tasks and more time focusing on what really matters."

After the demonstration, employees were divided into small groups for hands-on practice. Each group was given a set of tasks to complete using the new software. Alex walked around, offering support and answering questions. "Don't hesitate to ask if you get stuck," Alex encouraged. "Learning is a process, and it's okay to make mistakes."

As the session progressed, it became clear that some employees were catching on faster than others. Sarah, a new team member, was struggling a bit. Seeing this, Alex offered extra assistance. "Sarah, let's go through this step-by-step together. It's important to understand the basics before moving on to more advanced features."

By the end of the day, the training session had covered all the essential aspects of the software. Alex wrapped up with a review. "Remember, learning this system is just the beginning. Technology is always evolving, and it's important to keep learning and adapting."

The employees left the training room with a mix of relief and excitement. They knew that mastering the new software would take some time, but they felt more confident about tackling the challenge. Emma reflected on the session. "I was nervous at first, but the training really helped me understand how this system will make our work easier."

The next few weeks were busy as employees continued to familiarize themselves with the new software. Alex checked in regularly, offering additional training sessions and answering questions. The company's investment in continuous learning paid off, as productivity increased and employees adapted smoothly to the new system.

TechWorld Inc. learned an important lesson: embracing new technology and committing to continuous learning were key to staying ahead in a rapidly changing world.

Introduction - The act of presenting or beginning something new.

The introduction of the new software system caused excitement among the employees.

Coordinator - A person who organizes and manages an event or project.

Alex, the training coordinator, was responsible for the software training session.

Demonstration - A practical showing of how something works.

Alex gave a detailed demonstration of the new software's features.

Dashboard - A user interface that displays key information and controls.

The dashboard is where you'll find all the key tools for your daily tasks.

Workflow - The sequence of processes through which a piece of work passes from initiation to completion.

The new system was designed to improve our workflow and efficiency.

Streamline - To simplify or make more efficient.

The system aims to streamline processes and reduce repetitive tasks.

Support - Assistance or help given to someone.

Alex offered support to employees who were having trouble with the software.

Encouraged - Given support or confidence to do something.

Alex encouraged everyone to ask questions and not be afraid to make mistakes.

Struggling - Having difficulty or facing challenges.

Sarah was struggling with some of the new software

features.

Assist - To help or give support to someone.

Alex offered extra assistance to Sarah to help her understand the software.

Basics - The fundamental principles or starting points of a subject.

It's important to understand the basics before moving on to advanced features.

Advanced - More complex or developed.

The training covered both basic and advanced features of the software.

Reflection - Thought or consideration about a previous experience.

Emma's reflection on the training session showed she felt more confident.

Productivity - The efficiency of work, measured by output.

Productivity increased as employees adapted to the new system.

Familiarize - To make oneself acquainted or knowledgeable about something.

Employees continued to familiarize themselves with the new software over the following weeks.

35.

THE OFFICE REDESIGN

At Global Solutions Ltd., the office was about to undergo a major redesign. The management team had decided that a fresh look and a more functional layout would boost productivity and create a better work environment. The news was met with a mix of excitement and uncertainty.

Jessica, the office manager, called a meeting to discuss the upcoming changes. "As you all know, our office will be undergoing a redesign starting next week. The goal is to create a more open and collaborative workspace. We want to make sure that everyone feels comfortable and productive in the new environment."

The team listened attentively as Jessica explained the plans. "We'll have new workstations with adjustable desks, more meeting rooms, and a lounge area where you can relax. The design will focus on creating a space that promotes teamwork and creativity."

Tom, from the IT department, raised a concern. "How will the redesign affect our daily work? Will there be disruptions?" Jessica reassured him, "We're working closely with the design team to minimize any interruptions. The construction will be done in phases so that we can continue working while the changes are being made."

Over the next few weeks, the office was a hub of activity. Construction crews moved in, and furniture was rearranged.

There was dust and noise, but the team adjusted to the changes as best as they could. Workstations were temporarily set up in the conference rooms, and employees were encouraged to use the new lounge area for breaks.

Sara, who was in marketing, found the transition challenging. "It's hard to concentrate with all the noise," she said. Jessica understood and offered a solution. "If you need a quieter place to work, we can set up a temporary quiet zone in one of the meeting rooms."

The redesign was completed on schedule, and the new office opened its doors. The transformation was impressive. The once cramped space was now open and airy, with comfortable workstations and bright, inviting colors. The new layout included collaborative spaces with whiteboards and comfortable seating.

The team gathered for a tour of the redesigned office. Jessica pointed out the new features. "Here's the lounge area where you can unwind during breaks. And this is the new brainstorming room, designed to spark creativity."

As the days went by, employees adapted to the new workspace. The open layout and collaborative areas fostered better communication and teamwork. The team found that they could work more efficiently and felt more engaged in their tasks.

Sara, who had initially struggled with the transition, was now positive about the changes. "The new office layout is great. I love the open spaces and the new meeting rooms. It's much easier to collaborate with my team."

Jessica was pleased with the outcome. "I'm glad to see that everyone is adjusting well. The redesign has made a big difference in our work environment, and it's great to see that it's boosting productivity and morale."

The office redesign had achieved its goal. The new workspace not only enhanced productivity but also created a more enjoyable and engaging environment for the team.

Redesign - The process of changing the appearance or layout of something.

- The office underwent a redesign to improve the work environment.

Workspace - The area where work is done, including desks and other work-related areas.

- The new workspace includes open areas and collaborative rooms.

Productivity - The efficiency of work, measured by output.

- The redesign aimed to boost productivity by creating a more functional workspace.

Layout - The arrangement of items or areas in a particular way.

- The new office layout includes adjustable desks and more meeting rooms.

Collaborative - Working together with others to achieve a common goal.

- The new office design promotes collaborative work with shared spaces and whiteboards.

Functional - Designed to be practical and useful.

- The office was redesigned to be more functional and comfortable.

Lounge - A comfortable area where people can relax or take breaks.

- The new lounge area is perfect for unwinding during breaks.

Disruption - Interruption or disturbance that affects normal operations.

- Jessica assured the team that disruptions would be minimized during the redesign.

Temporary - Lasting for a short period of time.

- Workstations were set up temporarily in the conference rooms.

Adjust - To change or adapt to new conditions.

- The team had to adjust to the temporary workspaces during the construction.

Phase - A stage in a process of change or development.

- The construction was done in phases to avoid major disruptions.

Impressive - Evoking admiration or respect.

- The transformation of the office was impressive, with its new open and airy design.

Engaged - Involved or interested in something.

- The new workspace made the team feel more engaged in their tasks.

Morale - The confidence, enthusiasm, and discipline of a group.

- The redesign improved the office morale, making the work environment more pleasant.

Adjustment - A change made to improve or adapt to new conditions.

- The adjustment to the new office layout was smooth, and the team quickly adapted.

36.

THE DIVERSITY WORKSHOP

At Stellar Enterprises, the HR department had organized a diversity workshop to help employees understand the importance of inclusivity and respect for different perspectives. The goal was to create a more inclusive workplace where everyone felt valued.

On the day of the workshop, the team gathered in the conference room. The facilitator, Mia, started the session with a warm welcome. "Thank you all for joining today's diversity workshop. We're here to learn how to appreciate and respect the variety of perspectives and backgrounds that make our team unique."

Mia began by explaining what diversity meant. "Diversity is about recognizing and valuing the differences between people. These differences can include race, gender, age, religion, and many other aspects of our identities. Embracing diversity helps us build stronger, more innovative teams."

The first activity involved sharing personal stories. Each participant took turns talking about their background and experiences. Sarah, from marketing, shared her story. "I grew up in a multicultural family. My parents come from different countries, and I've always enjoyed learning about different cultures."

Listening to Sarah, Tom from the finance team realized how much he had to learn about his colleagues. "I never really thought about how diverse our team is. This workshop is eye-opening."

Next, Mia led a discussion on inclusivity. "Inclusivity means making sure that everyone feels welcome and respected, regardless of their background. It's important to be aware of our own biases and work towards overcoming them."

The group then watched a short film that highlighted various scenarios where inclusivity made a difference. The film showed how small acts of kindness and understanding could create a positive impact in the workplace.

After the film, Mia encouraged the team to brainstorm ideas on how to foster inclusivity at work. "What are some actions we can take to ensure that everyone feels included?" The team discussed various strategies, such as offering flexible work hours, creating employee resource groups, and providing diversity training.

David, from the IT department, suggested, "We could start a mentorship program to support new employees from different backgrounds. It could help them feel more integrated into the team."

The workshop concluded with Mia summarizing the key points. "Diversity and inclusivity are essential for creating a positive and productive work environment. By respecting and valuing each other's differences, we can build a stronger, more collaborative team."

As the team left the workshop, many employees felt inspired to make a difference. They understood that embracing diversity wasn't just about policies; it was about building meaningful relationships and creating a supportive environment for everyone.

Jessica, a team leader, reflected on the day's activities. "The workshop was really valuable. I'm excited to see how we can apply what we learned to make our workplace more inclusive and welcoming."

The diversity workshop had successfully opened the team's eyes to the value of inclusivity, setting the stage for a more understanding and supportive workplace.

Diversity - The presence of different types of people in a group or organization.
- Embracing diversity helps us build stronger, more innovative teams.

Inclusivity - The practice of including people from all backgrounds and ensuring they feel welcome.
- Inclusivity means making sure everyone feels respected, regardless of their background.

Facilitator - A person who leads or organizes a discussion or activity.
- Mia, the facilitator, guided the workshop and helped everyone participate.

Perspective - A particular way of looking at or thinking about something.
- Understanding different perspectives helps us appreciate each other's experiences.

Background - The experiences and culture that shape a person's identity.
- Sarah shared her background of growing up in a multicultural family.

Bias - A tendency to favor or dislike something unfairly.
- It's important to be aware of our own biases and work towards overcoming them.

Scenarios - Different situations or examples used to illustrate a point.

- The film showed various scenarios where inclusivity made a difference.

Mentorship - Guidance and support provided by a more experienced person to help someone develop.

- David suggested starting a mentorship program to support new employees.

Resource Groups - Teams or organizations within a company focused on specific interests or backgrounds.

- Employee resource groups can help create a more inclusive work environment.

Polic - Rules or guidelines that govern behavior.

- The workshop emphasized that inclusivity isn't just about policies but about relationships.

Integrated - To become a part of a group or organization and be included in its activities.

- A mentorship program could help new employees feel more integrated into the team.

Supportive - Providing help or encouragement.

- The workshop aimed to create a supportive environment for all employees.

Engaged - Being actively involved and interested in something.

- The team felt more engaged after learning about the value of diversity.

Innovative - Introducing new ideas or methods.

- Embracing diversity can lead to more innovative solutions and ideas.

Meaningful - Having a significant or important impact.

- Building meaningful relationships is a key part of creating an inclusive workplace.

37.

THE TIME MANAGEMENT CHALLENGE

Lisa had always been busy. With work, study, and personal commitments, she felt overwhelmed. Her days were filled with tasks, but she often struggled to finish everything on her list. One day, Lisa decided that she needed to find a better way to manage her time.

She started by researching time management techniques online. One common method she found was prioritizing tasks. "It's important to know what needs to be done first," she read. Lisa decided to try this approach. She made a list of all her tasks and ranked them in order of importance.

Her first task was to tackle urgent assignments for work. Lisa often found herself working late into the night to meet deadlines. By prioritizing these tasks, she hoped to avoid last-minute stress. She set aside specific times each day to focus on these assignments and used a planner to keep track of her deadlines.

Lisa also learned about the importance of setting goals. "Setting clear, achievable goals helps you stay focused," one article suggested. She started setting small, daily goals for herself. Instead of saying, "I need to get everything done," she began saying, "Today, I will finish this report and call three clients."

To stay organized, Lisa tried using different tools. She used a calendar app to schedule her meetings and deadlines. The app sent her reminders, which helped her stay on track. Lisa also used sticky notes to keep track of quick tasks, like picking up groceries or sending an email.

One technique that Lisa found especially helpful was the "Pomodoro Technique." This method involves working for 25 minutes, then taking a 5-minute break. Lisa discovered that this approach made her work sessions more productive. After a few cycles, she felt refreshed and ready to tackle more tasks.

Lisa's friends noticed a change in her mood. She was less stressed and more confident. "I can't believe how much more I've accomplished," Lisa told her friend Jenna. Jenna was curious and asked Lisa to share her new time management strategies.

Lisa explained, "It's all about finding what works best for you. Prioritize your tasks, set clear goals, use tools to stay organized, and try different techniques to see what helps you stay focused."

Over time, Lisa became more skilled at managing her time. She found a balance between her work, study, and personal life. By using the techniques she had learned, Lisa felt more in control and less overwhelmed. Her days were now filled with productivity and satisfaction.

Overwhelmed - Feeling like you have too much to handle or manage.
- Lisa felt overwhelmed by her many responsibilities.

Prioritize - To arrange tasks in order of importance.
- She made a list and prioritized her tasks for the day.

Urgent - Requiring immediate attention or action.
- Lisa focused on urgent assignments to meet her deadlines.

Deadlines - The times by which something must be completed.
- Using a planner helped Lisa keep track of her deadlines.

Achievable - Possible to accomplish or reach.
- Setting clear, achievable goals helps you stay focused.

Reminders - Notifications or cues to help remember something.
- The calendar app sent Lisa reminders about her meetings.

Productive - Making a lot of progress or achieving a lot.
- The Pomodoro Technique made Lisa's work sessions more productive.

Stress - A state of mental or emotional strain.
- Lisa was less stressed after learning time management techniques.

Tool - A device or method used to accomplish a task.
- Lisa used a calendar app and sticky notes as tools to stay organized.

Balance - A state where different elements are equal or in the right proportions.
- Lisa found a balance between her work, study, and personal life.

Sessions - Periods of time dedicated to a specific activity.
- She worked for 25 minutes in each Pomodoro session.

Refreshed - Feeling rejuvenated or more energetic after a break.
- After a few cycles of the Pomodoro Technique, Lisa felt refreshed.

Confident - Feeling sure of oneself and one's abilities.
- Lisa was more confident and less stressed after improving her time management.

Strategy - A plan or method for achieving a goal.

- Lisa shared her time management strategies with her friend.

Techniques - Methods or ways of doing something.

- She learned various time management techniques and found what worked best for her.

38.

THE CUSTOMER SURVEY

The team at GreenTech Solutions had been working hard to improve their products and services. However, they weren't sure if their efforts were making a difference. To find out, they decided to conduct a customer survey.

"Surveys are a great way to gather feedback from our customers," said Mark, the team leader. "We need to understand what our clients think about our products and services."

The team spent several days designing the survey. They created questions that would help them learn more about customer satisfaction, product quality, and areas for improvement. "It's important that our questions are clear and easy to understand," said Sarah, the marketing specialist. She wanted to ensure that customers could answer the questions without confusion.

Once the survey was ready, the team sent it out to their customers via email. They also included a link to the survey on their website and social media platforms. "The more responses we get, the better our data will be," Mark explained.

Over the next few weeks, the team received hundreds of responses. They carefully analyzed the data to find common trends and patterns. "We're looking for feedback that can help us improve," Sarah noted. She and her colleagues used charts and graphs to visualize the data, making it easier to understand.

The survey results showed that many customers were happy

with the product's performance but felt that the customer service could be improved. "It's clear that we need to focus on our customer service," Mark said. "We can use this feedback to make our services better."

The team held a meeting to discuss the results and plan their next steps. They decided to provide additional training for their customer service representatives and implement new procedures to address common issues. "Improving our customer service will help us build stronger relationships with our clients," Sarah said.

As they worked on the changes, the team kept their customers informed about the improvements. They sent follow-up emails and updates on their website. "We want our customers to know that we value their feedback and are taking action," Mark said.

In the end, the customer survey proved to be a valuable tool for GreenTech Solutions. It helped them identify areas for improvement and make changes that benefited their clients. "Surveys are a powerful way to gather insights and make informed decisions," Sarah concluded.

Survey - A set of questions used to gather information from people.

- The team sent out a survey to understand customer satisfaction.

Feedback - Information about reactions to a product or service used as a basis for improvement.

- The feedback from the survey showed that many customers were satisfied with the product.

Satisfaction - The feeling of contentment or happiness with something.

- Many customers expressed satisfaction with the product's performance.

Quality - The standard of something as measured against other things.

- The survey helped the team assess the quality of their services.

Confusion - A lack of clarity or understanding.

- Sarah wanted to ensure that the questions were clear to avoid confusion.

Responses - Answers or replies to a survey or question.

- The team received hundreds of responses to their survey.

Analyze - To examine data carefully to understand it better.

- The team analyzed the survey data to find common trends.

Trends - General directions or patterns in data.

- They looked for trends in the survey results to identify areas for improvement.

Patterns - Regular and repeated arrangements or sequences in data.

- The data revealed patterns that highlighted issues with customer service.

Improvement - The process of making something better.

- The team decided to focus on customer service improvement based on survey results.

Training - The process of teaching or learning skills.

- They planned to provide additional training for customer service representatives.

Procedures - Established methods or steps for doing something.

- New procedures were implemented to address common customer issues.

Relationships - Connections or interactions between people.

- Improving customer service would help build stronger relationships with clients.

Informed - Having or showing knowledge of something.

- The team kept their customers informed about the improvements.

Insights - Understanding gained from analyzing data or information.

- The survey provided valuable insights into customer needs and preferences.

39.

THE CORPORATE SOCIAL RESPONSIBILITY PROJECT

At BrightFuture Technologies, the team was excited to start their new project: a corporate social responsibility (CSR) initiative. This project aimed to give back to the community and make a positive impact.

During their first meeting, Lisa, the project manager, explained, "Our goal is to choose a cause that we can support as a company. This project will not only help those in need but also bring us closer together as a team."

The employees brainstormed various ideas for their CSR project. Some suggested organizing a charity run, while others thought about partnering with local schools to provide educational resources. After discussing their options, they decided to focus on improving the local community center.

"The community center is a great choice," said John, a senior developer. "It's a place where people of all ages come together, and it could really use some help."

The team began by visiting the community center to assess its needs. They found that the center needed new furniture, better lighting, and a fresh coat of paint. "We can tackle these tasks in stages," Lisa suggested. "First, let's start with the furniture."

The employees divided into groups to handle different tasks. Some were responsible for fundraising, while others organized volunteer work. Emily, who was in charge of fundraising, set up an online campaign and reached out to local businesses for donations. "We need to raise enough money to cover the costs of the new furniture and supplies," she explained.

Meanwhile, the volunteer group prepared for the renovation work. They painted walls, assembled new furniture, and improved the lighting. "It's amazing to see how a little effort can make such a big difference," said Michael, a team member who loved hands-on work.

As the project progressed, the team saw the community center transform. The new furniture and bright colors created a welcoming atmosphere. The community members were thrilled with the changes. "Thank you so much for your help," said Mrs. Carter, the center's director. "The improvements mean a lot to us."

The project was a huge success, and the team felt proud of their work. "It's rewarding to see the positive impact we've made," Lisa said. "We've not only helped the community but also strengthened our teamwork and commitment."

The CSR project taught the employees valuable lessons about giving back and the importance of working together. "We've learned that even small actions can have a big impact," John remarked. "It's a great feeling to contribute to something meaningful."

BrightFuture Technologies continued to support the community center and looked for new ways to engage in social responsibility. "We're excited about future projects and making a difference wherever we can," Lisa concluded.

Responsibility - A duty or obligation to do something.

- Taking on a CSR project is an important responsibility for the company.

Initiative - A new plan or project intended to achieve a goal.

- The CSR initiative aimed to improve the community center.

Impact - The effect or influence of something.

- The project had a positive impact on the community center.

Cause - A reason or purpose for which something is done.

- The team chose to support a cause that benefits the local community.

Assessment - The evaluation or estimation of the nature, quality, or ability of something.

- The team conducted an assessment of the community center's needs.

Fundraising - The act of collecting money for a cause or project.

- Emily organized a fundraising campaign to support the project.

Volunteer - A person who offers to do work without being paid.

- Volunteers helped with painting and assembling furniture at the community center.

Renovation - The process of improving or updating a building.

- The renovation work included painting walls and installing new furniture.

Transform - To change something significantly.

- The community center was transformed with new

furniture and bright colors.

Welcoming - Friendly or inviting.

- The new furniture and colors created a welcoming atmosphere in the community center.

Thrilled - Very pleased or excited.

- The community members were thrilled with the improvements.

Commitment - A promise or dedication to a cause or activity.

- The project strengthened the team's commitment to social responsibility.

Contribute - To give or add something to help achieve a goal.

- The employees contributed their time and effort to the project.

Meaningful - Important or significant.

- The project was a meaningful way to help the community.

Engage - To participate or become involved in something.

- The company looked for new ways to engage in social responsibility projects.

40.

THE PUBLIC RELATIONS CRISIS

At Horizon Innovations, things were running smoothly until one day when a serious issue arose. A social media post that was meant to promote their new product was misinterpreted and caused a public relations (PR) crisis. The company's reputation was suddenly at risk.

The PR team, led by Sarah, had to act quickly. Sarah called an emergency meeting with her team. "We need to address this situation immediately," she said. "Our priority is to manage the fallout and restore our reputation."

First, Sarah's team gathered all the facts about the incident. They learned that the post had been taken out of context and was causing widespread confusion. "We must issue a clear and honest statement to explain what happened," Sarah suggested. "It's important to be transparent with our audience."

The team worked on drafting a statement that would clarify the misunderstanding. They made sure to express their apologies for any offense caused and to explain the intent behind the original post. "Apologizing sincerely is crucial," said Mike, a team member. "We need to show that we understand the issue and are committed to making it right."

Once the statement was ready, it was time to address the media. Sarah and her team organized a press conference to answer questions and provide more information. "This will help us control the message and show that we are handling the situation responsibly," Sarah explained.

During the press conference, Sarah spoke confidently, answering questions and providing clear explanations. The media appreciated the company's proactive approach and willingness to address the issue openly. "Being transparent and responsive helps rebuild trust," Sarah noted.

The company also decided to engage with their customers directly. They used social media platforms to address concerns and answer questions from the public. "Engaging with our customers shows that we value their feedback and are dedicated to resolving the problem," said Emma, another team member.

As the days went by, the situation began to improve. The company's honest and proactive response helped to repair their reputation. "We've managed to turn a difficult situation into an opportunity to show our commitment to our customers," Sarah said.

In the end, Horizon Innovations learned valuable lessons about crisis management and the importance of clear communication. "Handling a PR crisis effectively requires quick action and transparency," Sarah concluded. "We're now better prepared for any future challenges."

Crisis - A time of intense difficulty or danger.

- The company faced a PR crisis when a social media post caused confusion.

Reputation - The beliefs or opinions that are generally held about someone or something.

- The company's reputation was at risk due to the misunderstood post.

Manage - To be in charge of or control something.

- The PR team had to manage the fallout from the crisis.

Fallout - The negative consequences or effects of an action.

- The team worked hard to manage the fallout from the PR crisis.

Transparent - Honest and open, not hiding anything.

- Issuing a clear statement is important to be transparent with the audience.

Apologize - To express regret for a mistake or wrongdoing.

- The company issued an apology for any offense caused by the post.

Sincerely - In a genuine and heartfelt way.

- Apologizing sincerely helps to show that the company understands the issue.

Proactive - Taking action in advance to prevent problems.

- Sarah organized a press conference to take a proactive approach to the crisis.

Engage - To interact or become involved with something.

- The company used social media to engage with their customers directly.

Rebuild - To restore or improve something that was damaged.

- The company's honest response helped to rebuild their reputation.

Clarify - To make something clear or easier to understand.

- The statement was meant to clarify the misunderstanding about the post.

Intent - The purpose or reason behind an action.

- The company explained the intent behind the original social media post.

Responsive - Reacting quickly and positively.

- Being responsive to media questions helps control the message during a crisis.

Proactive - Taking action in advance to address potential problems.

- A proactive approach can help manage a PR crisis effectively.

Commitment - A dedication or obligation to a cause or activity.

- The company's commitment to resolving the issue was evident in their actions.

41.

THE MARKET RESEARCH

At InnovateTech, the team was excited to start their latest project. They were tasked with conducting market research for a new product launch. Emily, the project manager, gathered everyone for a meeting to discuss their approach.

"Understanding our customers is crucial," Emily said. "We need to learn about their needs and preferences to create a product that they will love."

The team started by brainstorming different methods for gathering information. "We could use surveys," suggested John, one of the analysts. "They're a great way to get direct feedback from potential customers."

Emily nodded. "Surveys are a good idea. We can ask questions about what features people want and what problems they're facing with similar products."

Next, the team decided to analyze market trends. "We need to look at what's popular right now," said Sara, the marketing specialist. "Trends can show us what people are interested in and help us make informed decisions."

John was responsible for designing the survey questions. "I'll make sure to include questions that will help us understand customer preferences and expectations," he said. "It's important to be specific so we get useful data."

Once the surveys were ready, the team distributed them

through various channels—social media, email newsletters, and their website. They also planned to conduct some face-to-face interviews to get more detailed feedback.

After collecting the responses, the team gathered to analyze the data. Emily and Sara reviewed the results and looked for patterns. "We're seeing a strong interest in eco-friendly products," Sara noted. "It's clear that sustainability is important to our customers."

The team also examined competitors to see what they were offering. "By comparing our findings with what's already out there, we can identify gaps in the market," John explained. "This will help us position our product effectively."

Based on their research, the team made several recommendations. They decided to focus on developing eco-friendly features and to highlight these in their marketing campaigns. "Our research shows that customers are willing to pay more for sustainable products," Emily said. "We should definitely emphasize this in our launch strategy."

The product was launched with great success, and the team's efforts paid off. "Conducting thorough market research was key to understanding what our customers want," Emily said. "It helped us create a product that really resonates with them."

The team learned valuable lessons about market research and its impact on product development. "We've shown how important it is to listen to our customers and stay updated on market trends," Sara concluded. "This knowledge will guide us in future projects as well."

Consumer - A person who purchases goods or services for personal use.
- Understanding consumer needs is important for creating products that people will love.

Preferences - The things that someone likes or prefers.

- The survey helped us understand customer preferences and expectations.

Trends - General directions in which something is developing or changing.

- Analyzing market trends can show what's popular and help make informed decisions.

Informed - Having or showing knowledge of a particular subject or situation.

- Market research helps us make informed decisions about product development.

Feedback - Information about reactions to a product or service used as a basis for improvement.

- Collecting feedback from surveys provides valuable insights into customer needs.

Eco-friendly - Not harmful to the environment.

- The team decided to focus on developing eco-friendly features for the new product.

Sustainability - The ability to be maintained at a certain rate or level, especially without damaging the environment.

- Customers are interested in products that emphasize sustainability.

Competitors - Other companies or people who offer similar products or services.

- By examining competitors, we can identify gaps in the market.

Position - To place or arrange something in a particular way or location.

- The team's research helped them position their product

effectively in the market.

Campaign - An organized series of actions intended to achieve a specific result.

- The marketing campaign highlighted the eco-friendly features of the new product.

Resonates - To produce or be filled with a deep, full, or rich sound or emotion.

- The product launch was successful because it resonated with the customers.

Develop - To grow or cause to grow and become more mature or advanced.

- The team focused on developing features that would appeal to their target market.

Identify - To recognize or be able to name someone or something.

- Research helps to identify gaps in the market and opportunities for new products.

Analyze - To examine something in detail to understand it better or to draw conclusions.

- Analyzing the survey results helped the team understand customer needs better.

Recommendations - Suggestions or advice on what to do.

- The team made recommendations based on their market research findings.

42.

THE OFFICE ERGONOMICS

At WorkWell Inc., employees were starting to feel the strain of long hours at their desks. Many complained about back pain, eye strain, and wrist discomfort. To address these issues, the company decided to introduce a workshop on office ergonomics.

Sarah, the HR manager, led the session. She started by explaining what ergonomics is. "Ergonomics is all about designing your workspace to fit your needs and keep you comfortable," she said. "It helps prevent injuries and improve your overall well-being."

The first topic was **posture**. Sarah demonstrated how to sit properly at a desk. "Your chair should support your lower back, and your feet should be flat on the floor," she said. "Your computer screen should be at eye level so you don't strain your neck."

Tom, an employee from the IT department, asked, "What about our keyboards and mice?"

Sarah responded, "Good question! Your keyboard should be at a height where your elbows are at a 90-degree angle. Your mouse should be close to your keyboard so you don't have to stretch your arm too much."

Next, Sarah talked about **breaks**. "It's important to take regular breaks to stretch and move around," she explained. "Sitting for long periods can lead to discomfort and health issues."

Mia, a graphic designer, said, "I often forget to take breaks. I get so absorbed in my work."

Sarah suggested, "Set a timer every hour to remind yourself to stand up and stretch. There are also exercises you can do right at your desk."

The workshop also covered **lighting**. Sarah advised, "Proper lighting is crucial to avoid eye strain. Make sure your workspace is well-lit, but avoid glare from windows or overhead lights."

James, from the marketing team, mentioned, "I have a lot of glare from my computer screen."

Sarah recommended using an **adjustable desk lamp** to reduce glare and improve visibility. "You can also adjust the brightness and contrast settings on your monitor to make it easier on your eyes."

Finally, Sarah emphasized the importance of a **healthy workspace**. "Keep your desk tidy and organized," she said. "A clutter-free area helps you stay focused and reduces stress."

By the end of the workshop, employees felt more informed about how to set up their workspaces for better health and comfort. "I learned a lot about how small changes can make a big difference," Tom said.

Sarah concluded, "Remember, ergonomics is about making your work environment work for you. Taking care of your body is key to staying productive and happy at work."

The employees left the workshop feeling motivated to apply what they had learned. "I'm excited to make these changes and see how they improve my comfort," Mia said.

Ergonomics - The science of designing a workspace to fit the needs of the user and prevent discomfort.

- Ergonomics helps prevent injuries and improve your overall well-being at work.

Posture - The way you sit or stand, especially in relation to your health.

- Your chair should support your lower back to maintain good posture.

Discomfort - A feeling of slight pain or unease.

- Regular breaks can help reduce discomfort from sitting for long periods.

Breaks - Periods of rest or pause from work.

- It's important to take regular breaks to stretch and move around.

Lighting - The way light is used in a workspace to avoid strain on the eyes.

- Proper lighting is crucial to avoid eye strain from working at a computer.

Glare - A strong, bright light that causes difficulty seeing.

- Using an adjustable desk lamp can help reduce glare from your computer screen.

Adjustable - Able to be changed or moved to fit different needs.

- An adjustable desk lamp can be positioned to reduce glare.

Workspace - The area where you work, including your desk and chair.

- Keep your workspace tidy and organized to stay focused and reduce stress.

Healthy - Promoting good health and well-being.

- Creating a healthy workspace is essential for your comfort and productivity.

Organized - Arranged in a systematic way to make things easier to find and use.

- A clutter-free, organized desk helps you stay focused and reduces stress.

43.

THE MENTORSHIP PROGRAM

At BrightTech Solutions, a new mentorship program was introduced to help new employees adjust to their roles. The idea was to pair each newcomer with a more experienced colleague who could guide them through their first few months.

Lena, a fresh graduate, was excited about starting her new job but felt a bit nervous. She was paired with Mark, a senior developer known for his expertise and patience. During their first meeting, Mark welcomed Lena warmly and explained how the mentorship program worked.

"This program is designed to help you settle in and learn the ropes," Mark said. "I'll be here to answer your questions and support you as you get used to the company's systems and culture."

Lena appreciated Mark's reassurance. "That sounds great! What should I expect during our meetings?"

Mark smiled and said, "We'll start with an overview of your role and responsibilities. Then, we'll focus on any challenges you're facing and work together on finding solutions. It's also a good opportunity for you to share your thoughts and feedback."

Over the next few weeks, Lena and Mark met regularly. Mark guided Lena through the company's software, introduced her to important contacts, and provided valuable advice on managing her workload. Lena found these sessions incredibly helpful.

One day, Lena encountered a problem with a project deadline. She was struggling to balance her tasks and felt overwhelmed. She reached out to Mark for advice.

Mark listened carefully and offered practical suggestions. "It sounds like you have a lot on your plate. Let's prioritize your tasks and break them down into smaller, manageable steps. Also, don't hesitate to ask for help from your colleagues if you need it."

Lena followed Mark's advice and managed to complete her project on time. She felt a sense of accomplishment and gratitude towards Mark. "Thank you for your support," she said. "I couldn't have done it without your guidance."

Mark responded, "I'm glad I could help. Remember, the mentorship program is here to support you, and we're all part of the same team. Don't hesitate to reach out whenever you need assistance."

As the months went by, Lena became more confident in her role. She started taking on more responsibilities and even began helping new team members herself. She realized how valuable the mentorship program had been in her growth and development.

Mark was pleased to see Lena's progress. "You've done an excellent job adjusting and growing in your role," he said. "It's been rewarding to see you develop your skills and confidence."

The mentorship program at BrightTech Solutions not only helped new employees like Lena feel more supported but also fostered a culture of learning and collaboration within the company. Everyone benefited from the exchange of knowledge and experience, making it a win-win for everyone involved.

Lena's experience demonstrated the importance of having a mentor to guide and support you through new challenges. It showed that with the right support, anyone could thrive in their new role and make a positive impact on their team.

Mentorship - A relationship in which a more experienced person helps guide someone less experienced.
- The mentorship program pairs new employees with experienced colleagues for guidance.

Colleague - A person you work with.
- Mark introduced Lena to important contacts and colleagues in the company.

Overview - A general summary of something.
- Mark gave Lena an overview of her role and responsibilities during their first meeting.

Responsibilities - Duties or tasks that you are expected to perform.
- Lena was learning how to manage her responsibilities with Mark's help.

Challenges - Difficult situations or problems that need to be addressed.
- Mark helped Lena overcome the challenges she faced with her project deadline.

Feedback - Information about how one is performing, used for improvement.
- Lena was encouraged to share her thoughts and feedback during their meetings.

Support - Assistance or help given to someone.
- Mark provided valuable support and advice to Lena as she adjusted to her new job.

Prioritize - To arrange or deal with things in order of importance.

- Mark suggested prioritizing Lena's tasks to manage her workload effectively.

Accomplishment - Something achieved successfully, especially through effort.

- Lena felt a sense of accomplishment when she completed her project on time.

Gratitude - A feeling of thankfulness.

- Lena expressed her gratitude towards Mark for his guidance and support.

Development - The process of growing or improving skills.

- The mentorship program helped Lena in her professional development and growth.

Confidence - Belief in one's own abilities.

- Lena became more confident in her role as she progressed with Mark's help.

Responsibilities - Tasks or duties that are assigned to someone.

- Lena was able to manage her responsibilities more effectively after receiving advice from Mark.

44.

THE INNOVATION CHALLENGE

At TechForward Inc., a new initiative called the Innovation Challenge was announced. The company wanted to encourage employees to think creatively and come up with new ideas to improve their products and services. The goal was to inspire fresh thinking and innovative solutions that could benefit the business.

Jenna, a junior designer, was both excited and nervous about participating in the challenge. She had always enjoyed brainstorming and coming up with new ideas, but this was her first time taking part in a company-wide competition.

During the kickoff meeting, the team gathered in the conference room to learn more about the challenge. Michael, the project leader, explained the details. "The Innovation Challenge is an opportunity for all of you to showcase your creativity. We're looking for innovative ideas that can help us enhance our products, streamline our processes, or improve customer experience."

Jenna's colleague, Sam, raised his hand. "How will the ideas be evaluated?"

Michael smiled and replied, "We have a panel of judges who will review each submission. They'll consider originality, feasibility, and potential impact. The top ideas will be presented to the company's leadership, and the winners will receive exciting prizes."

As soon as the meeting ended, Jenna and her team gathered to brainstorm. They started by discussing various problems they had encountered with their current products. Jenna suggested focusing on customer feedback to identify areas for improvement.

"I think we should look at the recent customer reviews," Jenna said. "There might be recurring issues or suggestions that could spark some innovative ideas."

The team agreed and spent the next few days analyzing customer feedback and brainstorming potential solutions. They came up with several ideas, but one in particular stood out. It was a new feature for their main product that could significantly enhance user experience.

Jenna's team worked hard to develop a prototype of the new feature. They spent long hours refining their idea, testing its functionality, and preparing a presentation for the judges. The team was excited but also a bit anxious about the upcoming presentation.

On the day of the presentation, Jenna felt her nerves. As she stood in front of the panel, she took a deep breath and began her pitch. She explained their idea clearly and demonstrated how it would improve the product. The judges listened intently and asked thoughtful questions.

When the results were announced, Jenna's team was thrilled to learn that their idea had won first place. They were rewarded with a trophy and a generous prize, but more importantly, their idea was going to be implemented in the company's next product release.

Jenna felt a great sense of accomplishment. "This challenge was a fantastic experience," she said. "It pushed us to think creatively and work together. I'm proud of what we achieved."

The Innovation Challenge had successfully encouraged the team to explore new ideas and think outside the box. It highlighted the importance of creativity in driving business growth and improving products. Jenna's team had not only contributed to the company's success but also learned valuable lessons about innovation and teamwork.

Innovation - The act of introducing new ideas or methods.

- The Innovation Challenge aimed to spark new ideas and improvements for the company's products.

Challenge - A task or problem that tests someone's abilities.

- The Innovation Challenge was a chance for employees to test their creativity and problem-solving skills.

Creativity - The ability to create new and original ideas.

- Jenna's creativity helped her team come up with a unique solution for the product.

Brainstorming - The process of generating a variety of ideas to solve a problem.

- The team spent several hours brainstorming to find the best solution for their project.

Prototype - An early model of a product used to test and develop ideas.

- Jenna's team developed a prototype of their new feature to demonstrate its potential.

Feasibility - The practicality or possibility of something being achieved.

- The judges evaluated the feasibility of each idea to determine if it could be successfully implemented.

Impact - The effect or influence of something.

- The new feature was expected to have a positive impact on user experience.

Submission - The act of presenting an idea or proposal for consideration.

- Each team's submission was reviewed by the panel of judges.

Accomplishment - Something achieved through effort and skill.

- Jenna felt a great sense of accomplishment when her team's idea won the challenge.

Panel - A group of people chosen to judge or discuss something.

- The panel of judges reviewed all the ideas and selected the best ones.

Feedback - Information about how well something is done, used for improvement.

- Analyzing customer feedback helped Jenna's team come up with their innovative idea.

Recurring - Happening repeatedly or frequently.

- The team noticed recurring issues in customer reviews that inspired their new feature.

Presentation - A formal display or explanation of an idea or project.

- Jenna prepared a detailed presentation to showcase their prototype to the judges.

Generous - Willing to give more than is usual or expected.

- The winners of the challenge received a generous prize for their innovative ideas.

Implemented - Put into effect or action.

- Jenna's team was excited that their winning idea would be implemented in the next product release.

45.

THE OFFICE CHARITY DRIVE

At the beginning of the month, TechForward Inc. announced an exciting new project: the Office Charity Drive. The goal was to collect donations for a local charity that supported underprivileged families. The company hoped to involve every employee in this meaningful initiative.

The announcement came during the weekly team meeting. Maria, the project coordinator, stood up to explain the details. "We're starting a charity drive to support our community. We'll be collecting non-perishable food items, clothing, and toys. Every department will have a collection box, and we need volunteers to help organize and sort the donations."

The team was enthusiastic. Alex, who worked in marketing, was eager to get involved. "This is a great opportunity to give back," he said. "I think it would be fun to organize some fundraising events to help boost our collection efforts."

Maria agreed and encouraged everyone to come up with ideas. Soon, the team brainstormed various activities, including a bake sale, a raffle, and a talent show. Each department took on different tasks, and everyone was excited about working together.

In the following weeks, the office buzzed with activity. The marketing team set up a colorful poster campaign to raise awareness about the charity drive. They designed eye-catching flyers and displayed them in common areas. The sales team organized the bake sale, baking cookies, cakes, and other treats to sell during lunch breaks.

Lisa from the finance department coordinated the raffle. She worked hard to gather donations from local businesses for raffle prizes. The talent show was also a big hit, with employees showcasing their various skills, from singing to magic tricks.

As the collection boxes filled up, the sense of community grew stronger. Employees came together to sort and pack the donations, ensuring everything was ready for delivery. The excitement was palpable as the team prepared for the final drop-off at the charity's headquarters.

On the day of the delivery, everyone gathered to load the donations into the van. Maria and Alex, along with a few volunteers, drove to the charity's location. The charity staff welcomed them with gratitude and quickly began sorting the items.

"It's amazing to see all the contributions," said Maria. "Our office really came together for this cause."

Alex nodded. "It's inspiring to see the difference we can make when we work as a team."

The Office Charity Drive was a success, not only in terms of the amount of donations collected but also in strengthening the bonds among employees. Everyone felt a sense of accomplishment and pride in their contributions.

By the end of the month, the team had learned valuable lessons about teamwork, community involvement, and the impact of giving. The experience had brought them closer together and highlighted the power of collective effort in making a positive change.

Charity - An organization that helps people in need or the act of giving to help others.

- The Office Charity Drive aimed to support a local charity that assists underprivileged families.

Donation - Something given to help others, often money or goods.

- Employees collected donations such as food, clothing, and toys for the charity.

Volunteer - A person who offers to help without being paid.

- Volunteers helped organize and sort the donations during the charity drive.

Fundraising - Activities done to collect money for a cause or charity.

- The team organized a bake sale and a raffle as part of their fundraising efforts.

Organize - To arrange or put things in order for a particular purpose.

- Alex and his team organized several events to support the charity drive.

Awareness - Knowledge or understanding of a particular situation or issue.

- The marketing team created posters to raise awareness about the charity drive.

Raffle - A lottery in which people buy tickets for a chance to win prizes.

- Lisa coordinated the raffle, collecting prizes donated by local businesses.

Contribution - Something that is given or done to help achieve a goal.

- Each employee's contribution to the charity drive was greatly appreciated.

Accomplishment - Something achieved through effort and hard work.

- The team felt a great sense of accomplishment after successfully organizing the charity drive.

Headquarters - The main office or central location of an organization.

- The donations were delivered to the charity's headquarters for distribution.

Gratitude - A feeling of thankfulness.

- The charity staff expressed their gratitude for the generous donations.

Inspiring - Motivating or encouraging.

- The team found the charity drive inspiring, seeing the impact of their efforts.

Bond - A strong connection or relationship between people.

- The charity drive helped strengthen the bond among employees.

Collective - Done by or involving a group of people working together.

- The collective effort of the office made a significant difference for the charity.

Impact - The effect or influence of something.

- The charity drive had a positive impact on the community and the employees.

46.

THE HEALTH AND SAFETY TRAINING

At TechForward Inc., it was time for the annual Health and Safety Training session. Every employee was required to attend, as it was crucial for ensuring workplace safety and preparing for emergencies. The training was scheduled for a Tuesday afternoon, and everyone was eager to learn more about staying safe at work.

As employees gathered in the conference room, Maria, the safety officer, began the session. She started by explaining the importance of health and safety in the workplace. "Our goal is to make sure everyone understands how to protect themselves and others while at work," Maria said. "Today, we'll cover emergency procedures, first aid, and how to avoid common workplace hazards."

The first topic was emergency procedures. Maria explained what to do in case of a fire. "If you hear the fire alarm, don't panic. Leave the building calmly and use the nearest exit. Don't use the elevators, as they may become unsafe during a fire." She also demonstrated how to use a fire extinguisher, showing the team how to aim, squeeze, and sweep the device to put out a small fire.

Next, Maria covered first aid basics. She talked about treating minor injuries like cuts and burns. "Always clean the wound with water and apply an antiseptic to prevent infection," she instructed. She also emphasized the importance of knowing how to perform CPR in case of a medical emergency. "CPR can save lives, so it's important to learn the proper techniques," Maria added.

The session continued with a discussion on workplace hazards. Maria pointed out common risks such as slippery floors, heavy equipment, and ergonomic issues. "Be cautious around wet floors and always use safety equipment when handling heavy objects," she advised. She also talked about maintaining good posture to avoid strain and injury.

To make the training engaging, Maria included interactive activities. Employees participated in role-playing scenarios where they practiced responding to emergencies and providing first aid. They also took a quiz to test their knowledge about workplace safety.

By the end of the session, everyone felt more confident about handling potential hazards and emergencies. Maria concluded with a reminder. "Safety is everyone's responsibility. If you see something unsafe, report it immediately. Together, we can ensure a safe and healthy workplace for all."

As the employees left the conference room, they appreciated the practical information they had learned. The Health and Safety Training had been informative and useful, equipping them with the skills needed to handle various situations and maintain a safe work environment.

Emergency - A serious situation requiring immediate action.

- In case of an emergency, use the nearest exit to leave the building.

Procedure - A set of actions or steps to follow in a specific situation.

- Maria explained the emergency procedures for dealing with a fire.

Hazard - A potential source of danger or risk.

- Common workplace hazards include slippery floors and heavy equipment.

Extinguisher - A device used to put out fires.

- Maria demonstrated how to use a fire extinguisher to put out a small fire.

Antiseptic - A substance used to prevent infection in wounds.

- Always clean the wound with water and apply an antiseptic to prevent infection.

CPR - Cardiopulmonary resuscitation, a life-saving technique used in emergencies.

- Learning CPR can be crucial for saving lives in medical emergencies.

Injury - Physical harm or damage to the body.

- Knowing how to treat minor injuries like cuts and burns is important for workplace safety.

Ergonomic - Relating to the design of equipment to improve comfort and prevent injury.

- Maintaining good ergonomic practices helps avoid strain and injury from poor posture.

Interactive - Involving active participation and engagement.

- The training included interactive activities like role-playing to make it more engaging.

Posture - The position in which you hold your body while sitting or standing.

- Good posture is important to avoid strain and injury while working.

Strain - Physical or mental stress or pressure.

- Proper ergonomic practices help prevent strain from long

hours of work.

Antiseptic - A substance used to prevent infection in wounds.

- Apply an antiseptic to a cut to avoid getting an infection.

Report - To inform or notify about something.

- If you see something unsafe, report it immediately to ensure everyone's safety.

47.

THE PERFORMANCE METRICS

At Synergy Solutions, the quarterly meeting was approaching, and the team needed to review their performance metrics. Sarah, the project manager, organized a special workshop to help everyone understand these important measurements.

"Good morning, team!" Sarah began as everyone settled into their seats. "Today, we're going to discuss performance metrics. These are the numbers and data we use to evaluate how well we're doing in our projects."

Tom, one of the senior analysts, took over to explain the basics. "Performance metrics are crucial for tracking our progress and making improvements. They help us see if we're meeting our goals and where we might need to adjust."

The team was eager to learn more. Sarah displayed a chart on the screen, showing different types of metrics. "Here we have several metrics, such as productivity, quality, and customer satisfaction. Each of these gives us insight into different aspects of our work."

Tom started with productivity. "Productivity measures how much work we're completing in a given time. For example, if we're finishing more tasks than planned, our productivity is high. But if we're falling behind, it's time to figure out why."

Next, Sarah talked about quality. "Quality metrics are about how well we're doing our work. This could be the accuracy of our reports or the effectiveness of our solutions. High quality means our work meets or exceeds the required standards."

The discussion then moved to customer satisfaction. "Customer satisfaction is a key metric," Tom explained. "It tells us how happy our clients are with our services. We can gather this information through surveys and feedback."

The team worked on an exercise where they analyzed sample data using these metrics. They calculated their productivity rates, evaluated the quality of their past projects, and reviewed customer feedback. This hands-on approach helped them understand how to apply metrics to real-life situations.

Sarah emphasized the importance of setting clear goals. "When we have specific targets, it's easier to measure success. For example, if we aim to increase customer satisfaction by 10% this quarter, we can track our progress and make adjustments if needed."

As the workshop concluded, the team felt more confident about using performance metrics. They understood that these measurements weren't just numbers but valuable tools for improving their work and achieving their goals.

"Remember," Sarah said with a smile, "performance metrics help us see where we are and guide us on where we need to go. Let's use them to continue growing and succeeding."

The team left the meeting room with a new perspective, ready to apply their knowledge and improve their performance. The workshop had made a complex topic much clearer and more manageable.

Metrics - Measurements or data used to evaluate performance.

- Performance metrics help us track our progress and measure success.

Productivity - The amount of work completed in a given time.

- High productivity means we're finishing more tasks than planned.

Quality - The standard or degree of excellence of work.

- Quality metrics are about how well we're doing our work.

Satisfaction - The feeling of contentment or pleasure from meeting expectations.

- Customer satisfaction tells us how happy our clients are with our services.

Adjust - To make changes to improve something.

- If we're falling behind, we need to adjust our plans to stay on track.

Evaluate - To assess or judge the quality or performance of something.

- We need to evaluate the quality of our past projects to see if we meet the required standards.

Insight - Understanding gained from analyzing data or information.

- Metrics give us insight into different aspects of our work.

Target - A specific goal or objective to aim for.

- Setting a target, like increasing customer satisfaction by 10%, helps us measure progress.

Survey - A method of gathering information from people, often through questions.

- We can gather customer satisfaction through surveys and feedback.

Feedback - Information or responses given to improve performance.

- Customer feedback helps us understand their satisfaction

and areas for improvement.

48.

THE COMPANY MERGER

When Innovative Solutions and Future Tech decided to merge, it was a big moment for both companies. Employees from both sides were excited but also a little anxious about what the change would bring.

The first day after the merger was filled with a buzz of activity. Sarah, who worked at Innovative Solutions, noticed a lot of unfamiliar faces. She was curious and a bit nervous about how things would change.

At the introductory meeting, David, the new CEO of the merged company, addressed everyone. "Welcome to the new company!" he said with a smile. "We're excited about the opportunities this merger brings. Our goal is to blend the best parts of both companies and create a stronger, more innovative organization."

David spoke about the new company culture. "We want to build a culture of collaboration and respect. It's important that we all work together and support each other as we adjust to the new processes."

Sarah met John, a team leader from Future Tech. John was friendly and eager to get to know his new colleagues. "It's great to meet you," he said. "I know change can be challenging, but we're all in this together. Let's make the most of it."

As the weeks went by, employees had to adapt to new processes and systems. There were different ways of doing things, and some people found it difficult to get used to the new methods. Training sessions were set up to help everyone learn the new procedures and technologies.

One afternoon, Sarah and her team had a meeting to discuss how the merger was affecting their work. They talked about the changes they had experienced and how they were handling the transition. Sarah shared her thoughts. "It's been a bit overwhelming, but I think we're starting to find our rhythm. It's helpful to have these discussions and share our experiences."

The HR department organized team-building activities to help employees get to know each other better. They arranged lunches, workshops, and social events. Sarah attended a workshop on effective communication, which she found useful for understanding her new colleagues' perspectives.

As time passed, the employees began to see the benefits of the merger. The new company was stronger and more diverse, offering a wider range of products and services. The combined expertise from both companies led to innovative solutions that impressed clients.

David and the leadership team continued to emphasize the importance of feedback. "Your input is valuable," David said. "We want to ensure that everyone feels comfortable and included as we move forward."

In the end, the merger proved to be a success. The employees had navigated the changes well, adapted to new ways of working, and embraced the new company culture. The collaboration between the two companies created a positive and dynamic work environment.

Sarah looked back on the experience with satisfaction. "It wasn't always easy, but the merger brought us new opportunities and a stronger team. I'm excited about what we can achieve together in the future."

Merge - To combine or join together.

- When Innovative Solutions and Future Tech decided to merge, it was a significant change for both companies.

Anxious - Feeling worried or uneasy.

- Sarah was a little anxious about how the changes would affect her work.

Culture - The shared values and behaviors of a group or organization.

- David spoke about the new company culture, emphasizing collaboration and respect.

Blend - To mix different elements together.

- Our goal is to blend the best parts of both companies to create a stronger organization.

Collaboration - Working together towards a common goal.

- We want to build a culture of collaboration where everyone supports each other.

Adapt - To adjust or change to fit new conditions.

- Employees had to adapt to new processes and systems after the merger.

Transition - The process of changing from one state to another.

- The team discussed how they were handling the transition to the new methods.

Training - The process of learning skills or knowledge for a job.

- Training sessions were set up to help everyone learn the new procedures.

Perspective - A particular way of thinking about something.

- The workshop on effective communication helped Sarah

understand her new colleagues' perspectives.

Diverse - Showing a great deal of variety; different.

- The new company was stronger and more diverse, offering a wider range of products and services.

Innovative - Introducing new ideas or methods.

- The combined expertise from both companies led to innovative solutions.

Input - Contributions or feedback given to help improve something.

- David emphasized the importance of feedback and said that everyone's input was valuable.

Satisfaction - The feeling of contentment when goals are met.

- Sarah looked back on the experience with satisfaction, pleased with how the merger turned out.

49.

THE PRODUCT LAUNCH EVENT

The team at Creative Solutions was excited about their upcoming product launch event. It was a chance to introduce their latest gadget to the public and showcase their hard work. Mia, the event coordinator, was responsible for organizing every detail to ensure the event went smoothly.

The first task was to plan the event. Mia and her team made a checklist of everything they needed: a venue, catering, decorations, and invitations. They chose a popular downtown location that could accommodate a large number of guests. Mia decided to hold the event in the evening to make it more accessible for people who worked during the day.

Next, Mia worked on marketing the event. She created eye-catching flyers and social media posts to generate buzz. The marketing team also reached out to local influencers to spread the word. "We want to make sure everyone knows about our launch," Mia said. "The more people we attract, the better the event will be."

On the day of the event, the team arrived early to set up. They arranged the space with stylish decorations that matched the product's theme. There were banners, balloons, and a large display showcasing the new gadget. Mia was pleased with how everything looked. "The decorations are perfect," she said, smiling.

As guests began to arrive, Mia and her team greeted them

warmly. They handed out welcome packets that included information about the product and a schedule of the evening's activities. The highlight of the event was a live demonstration of the gadget. The team had prepared a presentation that showed off the product's features and benefits.

During the presentation, Mia noticed that the audience was engaged and attentive. They asked questions and seemed genuinely interested in the new gadget. After the demonstration, the guests had a chance to try the product for themselves. Many were impressed by its innovative design and functionality.

Throughout the evening, Mia made sure to interact with the guests and gather feedback. She walked around, asking for their opinions and suggestions. "Your feedback is very important to us," she told them. "It helps us improve and make our products even better."

By the end of the night, the event was a success. The team had achieved their goal of generating excitement and interest in their new product. Mia was relieved and happy. "Everything went well," she said. "I'm proud of how the team came together and made this launch event a memorable experience."

As the guests left, they thanked the team for a fantastic evening. The positive response and enthusiastic feedback made all the hard work worthwhile. Mia and her team celebrated their success and began planning their next big project.

Coordinator - A person who organizes and manages events or activities.

- Mia, the event coordinator, was responsible for organizing every detail of the product launch.

Checklist - A list of items or tasks to be completed.

- They made a checklist of everything they needed for the

event: a venue, catering, decorations, and invitations.

Venue - The location where an event takes place.

- They chose a popular downtown venue that could accommodate a large number of guests.

Catering - Providing food and drinks for an event.

- The team arranged catering to provide refreshments for the guests at the launch event.

Invitations - Requests sent to people to attend an event.

- They sent out invitations to ensure that their target audience would attend the launch.

Marketing - Activities aimed at promoting and selling products.

- Mia worked on marketing the event by creating flyers and social media posts.

Buzz - Excitement and interest generated about something.

- The marketing team created buzz around the product launch to attract more people.

Decorations - Items used to make a space look attractive for an event.

- The space was arranged with stylish decorations that matched the product's theme.

Demonstration - A presentation showing how something works.

- The highlight of the event was a live demonstration of the gadget.

Engaged - Showing interest and involvement.

- Mia noticed that the audience was engaged and attentive during the presentation.

Feedback - Opinions and suggestions about something.

- Mia gathered feedback from guests to understand their opinions and improve future events.

Innovative - Featuring new and creative ideas.

- Many guests were impressed by the gadget's innovative design and functionality.

Relieved - Feeling comforted and less worried.

- Mia was relieved and happy when the event went well.

Memorable - Worth remembering; unforgettable.

- Mia was proud that the launch event was a memorable experience for everyone.

Enthusiastic - Showing intense and eager enjoyment.

- The positive response and enthusiastic feedback from the guests made the hard work worthwhile.

50.

THE ANNUAL REPORT

Every year, the team at Global Enterprises looks forward to preparing the company's annual report. This report is a crucial document that outlines the company's performance over the past year and provides insights into its financial health. This year, Emma, the lead accountant, was in charge of compiling the report.

Emma knew that preparing the annual report required careful attention to detail. First, she gathered all the necessary financial data. This included revenue, expenses, profits, and losses. "We need to make sure all the numbers are accurate," Emma reminded her team. "This report will be reviewed by our stakeholders and needs to be precise."

The team spent several weeks collecting and verifying data. They checked bank statements, invoices, and receipts to ensure that everything was correct. Emma also worked with the marketing and sales departments to include important information about the company's achievements and future plans. "It's not just about numbers," she said. "We need to highlight our successes and our goals for the coming year."

Once the data was gathered, the team began drafting the report. They created charts and graphs to make the information easier to understand. Emma wanted to ensure the report was not only informative but also engaging. "We need to present this information clearly," she said. "Our readers should be able to grasp the key points quickly."

Transparency was a key focus for the team. They made sure

to include detailed explanations of financial figures and any significant changes from the previous year. "Transparency is essential for maintaining trust with our stakeholders," Emma explained. "We need to show them how we've managed our resources and what we plan to do in the future."

The team also emphasized accountability. They provided an honest assessment of the company's performance, including areas where improvements were needed. "It's important to be honest about our challenges," Emma said. "This helps us build credibility and shows that we are committed to addressing any issues."

After several rounds of revisions, the report was ready for final approval. Emma and her team reviewed it one last time to ensure there were no errors. They then presented it to the company's executives, who were pleased with the result. "This is a comprehensive and well-presented report," the CEO said. "It reflects our dedication to transparency and accountability."

The annual report was then published and distributed to shareholders, employees, and other interested parties. Emma felt a sense of accomplishment as she saw the positive feedback from stakeholders. "It's rewarding to see our hard work pay off," she said. "The annual report is a key tool for communicating our success and our future plans."

As the team wrapped up the project, they began preparing for next year's report. Emma knew that the process would start all over again, but she was ready for the challenge. "Each year, we learn and improve," she said. "I'm looking forward to making next year's report even better."

Compiling - Gathering and putting together information.

- Emma was in charge of compiling the annual report for the company.

Revenue - The total amount of money received from sales or services.

- The report included details about the company's revenue and expenses.

Expenses - Costs incurred in the process of earning revenue.

- They analyzed the company's expenses to ensure accuracy in the report.

Profits - The financial gain after subtracting expenses from revenue.

- The report showed a significant increase in profits compared to the previous year.

Losses - Financial deficits when expenses exceed revenue.

- The team also reported on any losses the company experienced.

Achievements - Accomplishments or successes.

- Emma worked with the marketing team to highlight the company's achievements.

Goals - Objectives or targets to be achieved.

- The report included the company's goals for the coming year.

Charts - Visual representations of data.

- They created charts and graphs to make the financial information clearer.

Graphs - Diagrams showing relationships between different data points.

- The graphs helped illustrate the company's performance trends.

Transparency - Openness and clarity in reporting information.

- The team emphasized transparency to maintain trust with stakeholders.

Stakeholders - Individuals or groups interested in the company's performance.

- The annual report was distributed to shareholders, employees, and other stakeholders.

Accountability - Being responsible for one's actions and decisions.

- The report included an honest assessment of the company's performance and areas for improvement.

Credibility - The quality of being trusted and believed in.

- Being honest about challenges helped the company build credibility with its stakeholders.

Assessment - Evaluation or analysis of something.

- The team provided an assessment of the company's performance in the report.

Revisions - Changes made to improve or correct something.

- After several rounds of revisions, the report was ready for final approval.

www.ingramcontent.com/pod-product-compliance
Lightning Source LLC
Chambersburg PA
CBHW052144220526
45471CB00004B/1516